What is Deconstruction?

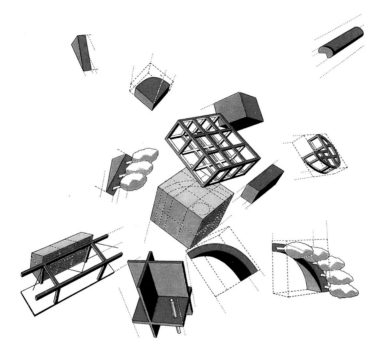

Bernard Tschumi

Zaha Hadid, Kurfürstendamm Office Building, Berlin, 1986-, Firewall Elevation

CHRISTOPHER NORRIS & ANDREW BENJAMIN

WHAT IS DECONSTRUCTION?

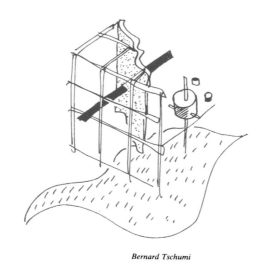

Bernard Tschumi

ACADEMY EDITIONS · LONDON / ST. MARTIN'S PRESS · NEW YORK

Acknowledgements
We would like to thank the following people and institutions for permission to reproduce works in this publication: Bernard Tschumi, front cover, pp.1, 3, 39; Zoe Zenghelis, back cover; Zaha Hadid, pp.2, 7, 32; Daniel Libeskind, p.5 (photo Uwe Rau), pp.33 and 46 (photo Hélène Binet); Peter Eisenman, p.6, 28 (above photo Dick Frank, below photo Wolfgang Hoyt), p.31, p.41 (photo Dick Frank); Morphosis, p.11 (above); Coop Himmelblau, p.11 (below); Office for Metropolitan Architecture, p.14 (photo Deutsches Architekturmuseum); Vincent van Gogh Foundation/National Museum Vincent van Gogh, Amsterdam, p.19; Jacques Derrida, Athelone Press, London/Chicago University Press, p.22; Courtesy Valerio Adami pp. 24, 45 (private collections, photos Gallerie Lelong); Courtesy William N. Copley Collection, New York, ADAGP Paris and DACS London, 1988, p.27; Günter Behnisch and Partner, p.37; Hiromi Fujii (photo Botond Bognar) p.40; Frank Gehry, p.43 (photo Mark C. Darley); Musée Fernand Léger, Biot, France, p.48; Courtesy Gérard Titus-Carmel and Galerie Lelong, p.49; Courtesy Cy Twombly, p.51; Courtesy Anselm Kiefer and (below) Saatchi Collection, London, and (above) Jerry and Emily Spiegel Collection, Kings Point, New York, p.52.

Front cover: Bernard Tschumi, Parc de la Villette, 1984-, superimposition. *Back cover:* Zoe Zenghelis, Parc de la Villette, 1985. *Page 1:* Bernard Tschumi, Parc de la Villette, 1984-, exploded folie. *Page 3:* Bernard Tschumi, Parc de la Villette, 1984-, ideogram.

Published in Great Britain in 1988 by
ACADEMY EDITIONS
an imprint of the Academy Group Ltd, 7 Holland Street, London W8 4NA

Copyright © 1988 Academy Editions, London

ISBN 0-85670-961-1

Published in the United States of America by
St. Martin's Press, 175 Fifth Avenue, New York, NY 10010

ISBN 0-312-02711-7

Printed and bound in Singapore

CONTENTS

Daniel Libeskind, City Edge, Berlin, 1987, site model A

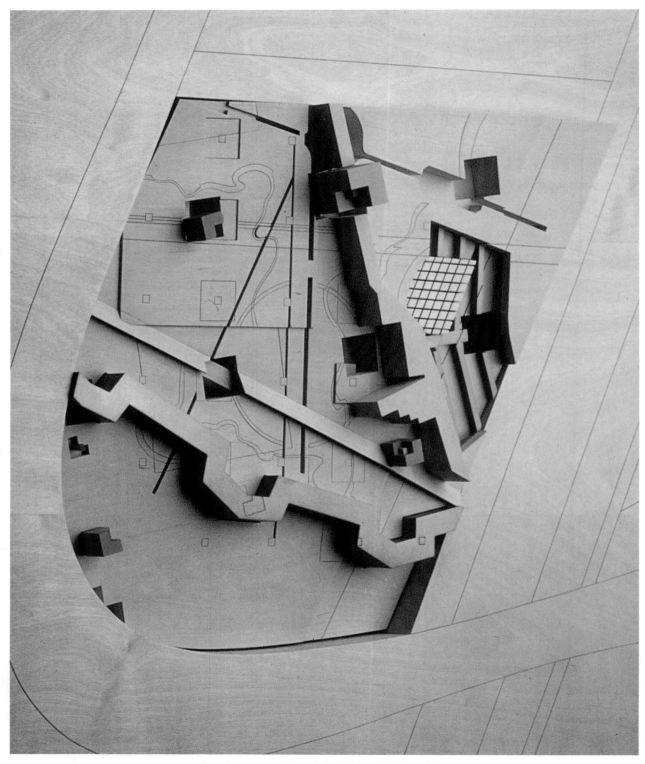

Peter Eisenman, Parc de la Villette, 1985, model

Deconstruction, Post-Modernism and the Visual Arts

CHRISTOPHER NORRIS

Zaha Hadid, Kurfürstendamm Office Building, Berlin, 1986-, Red Painting

The Metaphysics of Presence: Plato, Rousseau, Saussure

To 'deconstruct' a text is to draw out conflicting logics of sense and implication, with the object of showing that the text never exactly means what it says or says what it means. This approach was first developed by the French philosopher Jacques Derrida (born 1921), whose ideas were then taken up by numerous (mainly American) literary critics. Derrida's writings have been predominantly concerned with philosophical, rather than literary texts, although he would certainly reject the very terms of this distinction, arguing that philosophy – like literature – is a product of *rhetorical* figures and devices. What defines philosophy as a discipline, he argues, is precisely its reluctance to face this fact; its desire to ignore the omnipresence of figural language in the texts of its own past and present. Deconstruction is the process of rhetorical close-reading that seizes upon those moments when philosophy attempts – and signally fails – to efface all knowledge of this figural drift.

Thus Derrida reads philosophical texts very much against the grain of their overt meanings and intentions. He is proposing what amounts to a psychoanalysis of Western 'logocentric' reason, that reason which aims at a perfect, unmediated access to knowledge and truth. The 'unconscious' of philosophy – to pursue this comparison – could then be read in all the signs and symptoms of its own (long repressed) rhetorical dimension. This is why Derrida regards the opposition between *speech* and *writing* as among the most basic determinants of Western philosophical tradition. From Plato to Hegel, from Rousseau to Saussure and the modern (structuralist) sciences of man, speech is always privileged over writing, since spoken language is thought to possess a unique authenticity, a truthfulness deriving from the intimate relation between word and idea. [1] The ambiguity of the French phrase *s'entendre-parler* – meaning both 'to hear' and 'to understand oneself speak' – best conveys the logic of this potent belief. Speech enjoys priority by virtue of its issuing from a self-present grasp of what one means to say in the moment of actually saying it. And when we listen to the words of another such speaker, we are supposedly enabled to grasp their true sense by entering this same, privileged circle of exchange between mind, language and reality. Communication thus becomes ideally a kind of reciprocal 'auto-affection', a process that depends on the absolute priority of spoken (self-present) language over everything that threatens its proper domain. And *writing* constitutes precisely such a threat in so far as it is cut off at source from the authorising presence of speech. Writing is condemned to circulate endlessly from reader to reader, the best of whom can never be sure that they have understood the author's original intent. Its effect is to 'disseminate' meaning to a point where the authority of origins is pushed out of sight by the play of a henceforth limitless interpretative freedom.

Thus writing is condemned as a mere 'parasite', a debased, fallen mode of utterance, one that philosophers *must* perforce use (since otherwise their thoughts would be lost to posterity), but only on condition that they recognise these dangerous effects. To write is to risk having one's ideas perverted, wrenched out of context and exposed to all manner of mischievous reinterpretation. Socrates was wise enough to write nothing down but entrust his wisdom to a circle of initiates willing to listen and inwardly commemorate his words. Among those disciples was Plato, himself privileged (or condemned) to record *in writing* the various dialogues and scenes of instruction through which Socrates imparted his wisdom. There is an obvious irony in Plato's predicament, continuing as he does (in the *Phaedrus* and elsewhere) to denounce the wayward, subversive effects of writing, textuality or rhetoric. And this irony is yet more sharply underlined as Derrida brings out the strange double logic which comes into play whenever Plato touches on the vexed topic of written language.[2] For it seems that he is unable to argue his case for the superior truth-claims of speech without falling back on metaphors of writing – notably a mystic 'writing in the soul' – in order to explain how authentic wisdom comes about. These metaphors complicate the logic of Plato's dialogue beyond any hope of sorting them out into a clear-cut pattern of thematic development.

This kind of brief summary can scarcely do justice to Derrida's brilliant and meticulously argued account of the *Phaedrus*. But it does give some idea of the strategies involved in a 'classic' deconstructionist reading. One begins by locating those key-points in the text where its argument depends on some crucial opposition of terms, as between speech and writing. Then it is a matter of showing: 1. that these terms are hierarchically ordered, the one conceived as derivative from, or supplementary to, the other; 2. that this relation can in fact be inverted, the 'supplementary' term taking on a kind of logical priority; and 3. that the pattern of unstable relationships thus brought to light is characteristic of the text in every last detail of its rhetorical organisation. What Plato manifestly *means to say* is that writing is at best a poor substitute for speech and at worst a corrupter of authentic, first-hand wisdom. What his text actually turns out to mean – if read with an eye to this uncanny double logic – is that writing (or a certain idea of writing) is indispensable to philosophy and any reflection on the nature and limits of language.

In *Of Grammatology*, his best-known text, Derrida turns to Rousseau as a striking case of how these logical complications can inhabit an author's work and disrupt any semblance of unified, coherent sense.[3] Rousseau holds that *nature* is the pattern and the source of everything good in human life. As *culture* begins to develop – as societies evolve toward 'higher', more complex forms of organisation – so man loses touch with those primitive virtues. Language acquires more sophisticated means for expressing abstract ideas, but it also comes to lack any sense of its authentic (natural) origin in the speech-song of passionate feeling. In music, the spontaneous nature of *melody* gives way to a decadent modern style where *harmony* prevails, and where the multiplication of lines and notes demands that music be *written down*. Then there is the writing of Jean-Jacques himself, compulsively recounting his own life-history in the *Confessions* and guiltily aware of the constant temptation to falsify the record, disguise his faults, make himself appear a more complex, intriguing character. This bad habit exerts a contaminating influence, not least upon Rousseau's sexual indentity. In the 'natural' state of things, sex (like speech) is the passionate exchange of genuine, unselfconscious feeling between partners who perfectly reciprocate each other's desire. To indulge in auto-erotic fantasy or other kinds of solitary vice is for Rousseau a perversion of nature, a 'summoning up of absent beauties' that denies the living presence of sexual encounter. Like writing – and indeed as one effect of too much writing – this habit turns instinct from its natural path and induces all kinds of psychic disorder.

So writing is a 'dangerous supplement', the product of a decadent culture whose symptoms Rousseau discovers deep within and all around. In fact, as Derrida shows, this word 'supplement' appears with remarkable frequency whenever Rousseau is in the process of denouncing some further manifestation. But it is also a distinctly ambivalent word, and one whose double logic can again be shown to deconstruct all normative assumptions. On the one hand a 'supplement' is that which may be added to something already complete in itself and thus having no need of such optional extras. On the other, it is a necessary addition, one that supplies (makes up for) some existing lack and must henceforth be counted an integral part of the whole. The various 'supplements' to a standard work of reference like the *Oxford English Dictionary* might be taken in either sense, depending on whether the 'complete' *OED* is the original twenty-volume set or the set including its subsequent updates.

What Derrida discerns in Rousseau's text is the functioning of a 'supplementary' logic which repeats this curious twist of implication at every level. Thus Rousseau's theory of the origin of language – that it started as a kind of pre-articulate chant, then gradually declined into system and structure – breaks down as soon as he comes to examine its premises. Language can only communicate on the basis of shared conventions which in turn presuppose and articulate *systems* of distinctive sounds and meanings. Rousseau is sufficiently a structuralist *avant la lettre* to perceive, like Saussure, that a grasp of this system is prerequisite to any understanding of individual speech-acts. It is impossible to sustain the idea of a language so close to its primitive (natural) roots that no such effects would yet have overtaken its development.

A similar drastic reversal of values seems to befall those other loaded oppositions that characterise Rousseau's discourse. Society itself is strictly inconceivable except at a stage of historical advance far beyond its putative 'natural' origin. Quite simply, there is no social order – even the most primitive – which doesn't participate in 'culture' at least to the extent of displaying kinship-systems, distinctions of rank, codes of acceptable behaviour and so forth. What Rousseau *means to say* about the origins of society – that nature is the source of all human good – is effectively undone by what the logic of his text *constrains him to mean*. It is the same with his writings on music, where the notion of a pure melodic style – as yet untouched by the bad 'supplement' of harmony – cannot be sustained in the end. For melody is unthinkable except in terms of a certain harmonic context, a background of overtones, chordal progressions, implicit cadences, etc., which define our very sense of melodic continuity and shape. This applies even to a single (unaccompanied) vocal line, in so far as we perceive it to possess musical character. Once again, Rousseau is forced up against the limits of his nature/culture opposition; constrained to admit that there is always already a

'supplement' (or swerve from natural origins) perversely in at the source.

This is nowhere more apparent than in Rousseau's autobiographical writing. It is not simply that he has missed out on real-life experience by devoting so much time and effort to the reconstruction of his own past history. What is worse is the fact that this narrative – always ambivalently placed between truth and fiction – increasingly confounds any attempt to distinguish the one from the other. Rousseau confesses that he has always been awkward in company, unable to do himself justice by saying what he genuinely means and feels at any given time. His experience only comes alive, so to speak, in the act of writing it down, narrating what (supposedly) happened from a standpoint of idealised retrospective grasp. Thus Rousseau's *Confessions* take on this uncanny power to usurp the very nature and privileged value of real-life experience. Writing – that 'dangerous supplement' – perverts the natural order of things by substituting fictions and lifeless signs for the authentic living presence of speech. And this is most evident in the psychopathology of Rousseau's sexual desires, given over (as he ruefully confesses) to the realm of erotic fantasy and substitute pleasure. So far has he gone down this dangerous path that even the experience of 'natural' intercourse falls far short of his solitary dreams. Rousseau's instincts are perverted to the point where he needs to 'supplement' such real-life pleasures by imagining some other woman in the place of his actual, flesh-and-blood partner. And for Rousseau this habit is one more evil consequence of a writing that tends increasingly to blur the distinction between dream and reality.

What is remarkable in Derrida's readings of Plato and Rousseau is the way these effects become manifest at every level of the text. He is not simply offering new interpretations, or seizing on those passages that offer some hold for ingenious revisionist treatment. Derrida's claim is that language itself – or the language of Western 'logocentric' tradition – is always subject to the dislocating forces at work in these texts. On the one hand it is marked by that primordial 'metaphysics of presence' which subordinates writing in the name of an authentic, natural speech. On the other it bears involuntary witness to the conflicts, tensions and paradoxes created by a writing whose effects are everywhere inscribed within the language and history of Western culture. This 'writing' is not confined to the standard (restricted) definition which works to preserve the contrast between speech and secondary inscriptions, mere written marks on a page. In *Of Grammatology*, writing is the name of whatever resists the logocentric ethos of speech-as-presence. In the texts of that tradition it becomes a kind of scapegoat, a 'wandering exile', cast out from the garden of innocent, natural origins but exerting a constant disruptive pressure from the margins of discourse. Derrida employs the term *archi-écriture* to signify writing in this massively extended or generalised sense. Its domain thus includes the whole range of deplorable effects that Rousseau attributes to 'culture' as the active antithesis of everything genuine, spontaneous and natural in human affairs.

Two further examples may help to explain what Derrida is driving at here. When a modern anthropologist (Claude Lévi-Strauss) celebrates the virtues of a primitive life-style, it is *writing* that he sees as the chief corrupting influence thrust upon an innocent oral culture by the emissaries of Western civilisation (himself unhappily included).[4] The gift of writing is a double-edged, treacherous gift. It brings along with it the power to dominate others through possession of a secret, mandarin skill; the authority to lay down laws and prohibitions which are always those of a privileged class, and can thus be used to prop up a system based on arbitrary differences of rank. Writing becomes the precondition for every kind of social injustice that marks the progressive falling-away from a state of communal grace. And when a linguist (Saussure) asserts the priority of spoken over written language, it is likewise in terms of the corrupting effects that are brought about by substituting lifeless inscriptions for living sounds.[5] Speech is the proper, authentic form of language; writing not merely derivative from speech but in some sense a parasite, an alien body which exploits and perverts the very nature of language. It is the sheer exorbitance, the hyperbolic character of these charges against writing that Derrida asks us to recognise. Saussure and Lévi-Strauss are representative figures in a modern (structuralist) line of descent which undoubtedly looks back to Rousseau for its informing myths and values.

But their texts, like his, bear all the marks of an opposite, complicating tendency at work. Lévi-Strauss provides copious evidence that the tribe in question – the Nambikwara – already practised a great variety of laws, customs and social taboos which may not have been literally *written down*, but which yet had the force of articulate prescriptions. In short, these people were far from enjoying that state of idyllic communal existence that Lévi-Strauss identifies with the absence of writing. Once again, it is the Rousseauist mystique of origins that underwrites this notion of a small-scale, organic community, one where the face-to-face medium of speech suffices for all genuine social needs. If this were the case then writing would indeed be unable to assert its hold. But one only has to look more closely at Lévi-Strauss's text – at the detail of his trained ethnographic observation – to remark how many are the visible signs of a power that is exerted through the system of codified rules and regulations. And the same applies to Saussure's idea that the linguist should concentrate (at least as far as possible) on spoken rather than written language. For it is an axiom of Saussurian linguistics that meaning is the product of *differential* features – contrasts at the level of sound and sense – and not of any one-to-one identity between signifier and signified. And at certain crucial points in his argument Saussure falls back on analogies with writing as the best – perhaps the only – means to explain how this economy of difference operates. If modern linguistics has achieved some of its best results in analysing the sound-structure of language, this doesn't at all justify the phonocentric bias that equates 'natural' language with speech as self-presence and requires that writing be kept firmly in its place.

Framing the Text: Kant and Hegel

It will be seen, therefore, that deconstruction is first and foremost an activity of textual close-reading, and one that resists the kind of summary account which I am here trying to present. Derrida himself has made a point of refusing all requests for a snap definition. If there is one 'truth' about deconstruction, he asserts, it is the fact that no statement of the form 'deconstruction is x' can possibly claim any warrant or genuine explanatory power. Definitions are reductive in the sense that they assume some ultimate, one-for-one match between signifier and signified, some point at which the text (or the detailed activity of reading) would yield up a meaning ideally possessed of its own self-authenticating truth. And it is precisely this assumption that Derrida is out to subvert by insisting on the non-self-identical nature of the linguistic sign, its involvement in a process of unlimited semiosis (or *différance*) which cannot be arrested by any such stipulative limit.

'Différance' in French is a kind of strategic neologism compounded to the two verbs 'to differ' and 'to defer'.[6]

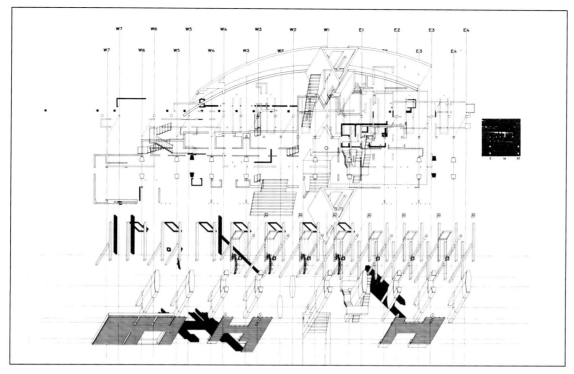

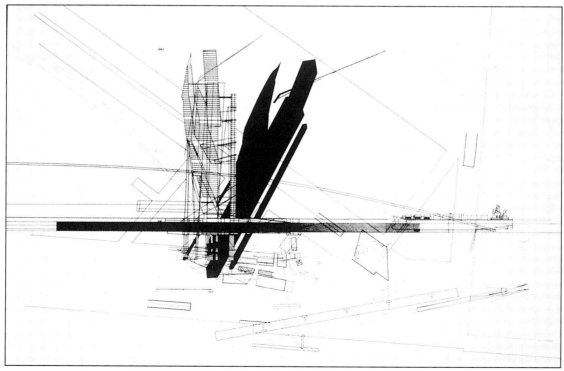

Above: Morphosis, Crawford Residence, Los Angeles, 1988, axonometric study
Below: Coop Himmelblau, Skyline Tower, Hamburg, 1985, site plan and section in axonometric

What it signifies – in brief – is the fact that meaning can never be accounted for in terms of punctual self-presence; that language is not only (as Saussure argued) a *differential* structure of contrasts and relationships 'without positive terms', but also that meaning is endlessly *deferred* along the chain of linguistic substitutions and displacements that occur whenever we seek to define what a given term signifies in context. It would therefore be wrong to treat the term 'deconstruction' as uniquely exempt from this general condition, or to offer a summary account of it as involving some pre-given sequence of arguments, strategies or moves. For this is to assume – against all the evidence of Derrida's writings – that concepts can exist in an ideal realm of self-identical meaning and value which somehow transcends the contingent fact of their existing in written or textual form. So one can well understand Derrida's impatience with those purveyors of short-cut intellectual fashion who demand to know what deconstruction 'is', how it works or what results it will standardly produce when applied to any text.

All the same it is possible to push too far with this purist attitude and ignore the very real *philosophical* cogency and rigour of Derrida's arguments. What he does most often – in a move familiar to philosophers at least since Kant – is interrogate the grounds (or 'conditions of possibility') that underwrite the truth-claims of this or that discourse. Take for instance his commentary on Husserl's essay 'The Origin of Geometry', where Husserl sets out to establish the fact that geometrical truths are ideal, that they exist – once discovered by a thinker like Euclid – in a realm of absolute, intuitive self-evidence, unaffected by the vagaries of written transmission.[7] What Derrida brings out through a close reading of Husserl's text is the way that his argument turns out to undermine (deconstruct) its own working premises. Hence the strict *impossibility* of conceiving geometry in terms of some primordial grounding intuition achieved repeatedly from age to age by everyone capable of grasping such truth. On the contrary, as Derrida argues: for truths to be 'ideal' in Husserl's sense it is necessary that they *not* be confined to the realm of intuitive self-evidence but conserved in a form of historically transmissible knowledge which writing alone is able to achieve. Indeed, Husserl himself (like Rousseau and Saussure) has passages that covertly acknowledge this necessity, even though he seeks to ground geometry in a realm of pure, self-present intuition where writing would figure as at most an ancillary device for reminding us of truths that we always in some sense already knew.

What Derrida is asking in each of the above cases (Plato, Rousseau, Saussure and Husserl) is something much akin to the Kantian question: namely, how it is possible for thinking to proceed at all when faced with certain ultimate problems in the nature of its own constitution as a self-reflective, self-critical project of enquiry. In Kant, these questions receive three kinds of answer according to the different forms or modalities of knowledge. *Understanding* is the province of epistemological critique, of a knowledge that deals with phenomena falling under the laws of objective cognition, causal explanation or other such perceived regularities of real-world experience. Its powers and limits are best established (Kant argues) by marking it off from all forms of speculative reason, all 'ideas' that go beyond any possible grounding in the data of intuitive self-evidence. So it is that, from the standpoint of theoretical understanding, 'intuitions without concepts are blind; concepts without intuitions are empty.' For *practical reason* (or ethics), on the contrary, what has to be preserved is the freedom or autonomy of human will, its capacity to legislate over actions and choices which must obey some ultimate categorical imperative, but which cannot be reduced to the level of natural necessity or rule-governed behaviour. Ethics is precisely that domain of reason where thinking gives itself the rule by appealing to a realm of 'supersensible' ideas whose source lies beyond all strictly theoretical understanding. And *aesthetic judgement* – his topic in the third *Critique* – has its own complex role to play in this Kantian structure of argument since it figures at crucial moments as a source of enabling transitions or analogies between one faculty and another.[8] Thus the 'Transcendental Aesthetic' is Kant's title for that section of the first *Critique* which explains how sensuous intuitions are brought under concepts in order to provide the essential link betwen experience and *a priori* knowledge.[9] And a similar connection exists between ethics and aesthetics, in so far as Kant seeks an analogy for moral law in our experience of art as calling forth powers of appreciative judgement that go beyond mere personal taste and demand universal assent.

Such knowledge cannot be legitimised in the manner of theoretical understanding, that is, by means of a cognitive appeal to objects of which we possess both a concept and a corresponding sensuous intuition. For it is, according to

Kant, the very hallmark of aesthetic judgement that it cannot be 'brought under' a concept or reduced to any set of necessary or sufficient properties attaching to the object itself. What the beautiful brings about – whether in nature or in art – is a 'free play' of the faculties wherein they discover a sense of harmonious cooperative balance unattainable through any other mode of experience. And the sublime comes yet closer to providing an analogue for the absolute, unconditioned character of ethical reason. It involves (as with many of the best-known passages in Wordsworth, Coleridge or Shelley) an essentially twofold movement of thought: a sense of the mind being at first overwhelmed by the sheer awesomeness of nature and its own incapacity to grasp or represent it, followed by the realisation that precisely this lack of any adequate objective correlative signals the existence of imaginative powers that go beyond the realm of phenomenal cognition to that of 'supersensible' ideas.[10] It is for this reason that Kant finds a kinship between ethics and that moment of sublime overreaching where intelligence responds to a call that would otherwise defeat all its powers of self-understanding.

It will help if we bear these arguments in mind when attempting to grasp how Derrida's work relates to the project of Kantian enlightened critique. Deconstruction is 'philosophical' in the sense that it deploys a distinctive mode of argument in raising certain problems about knowledge, meaning and representation. It suspends our commonsense-intuitive attitude and asks what ultimate grounds exist, in the nature of experience or *a priori* knowledge, for those items of belief we standardly take on trust. Moreover, it does this by always pursuing such judgements back a further stage, demanding what might be the 'conditions of possibility' that enable thought to get started on the process of examining its own claims to truth.[11] Thus Derrida will ask of Plato, Rousseau and Saussure: how is it that these thinkers can on the one hand denounce writing as a parasite, a 'dangerous supplement', an obtrusive and usurping substitute for speech, while on the other conducting their arguments through a whole series of analogies and metaphors whose covert referent is writing itself? Of course it must be true that speech precedes writing as a matter of historical development, at least in so far as writing is identified with that form of phonetic-alphabetical transcription which prevails within our own culture. But there is no good reason to suppose that this contingent fact about *some* languages can be erected into a generalised precondition for language in general. It is this habit of moving surreptitiously from *de facto* to *de jure* orders of argument, or from local observations to universal truth-claims, that Derrida finds everywhere at work in the texts of Western 'logocentric' tradition. Thus it is taken for granted by thinkers from Plato and Aristotle to Kant, Hegel, Husserl and Saussure that there exists a wholly natural order of priorities where ideas must first be articulated in speech and then – if neccessary – speech be recorded in the purely conventional and arbitrary signs that make up a written language.[12] Writing is seen as a bad necessity, a precondition for conserving and transmitting ideas from one generation to the next, but a recourse that can only be justified in so far as it obeys the imperative that *speech comes first*, and that writing must faithfully transcribe the elements of phonetic-alphabetical language.

This prejudice comes out with particular force in Hegel's insistence that no form of purely symbolic notation – no 'universal characteristic' of the kind proposed by a thinker like Leibniz – can possibly give rise to genuine, authentic philosophy.[13] For it is essential to Hegel's argument in the *Phenomenology of Mind* that thinking should proceed through a recapitulation of those various stages in its own prehistory that bear witness to a consciousness struggling to achieve the condition of lucid self-knowledge. This can only come about if the texts of that tradition give access to a realm of spiritualised conflicts and dramas whose expression may depend upon writing – since otherwise we would possess no record of them – but whose essential meaning must remain unaffected by the vagaries of written language. For Hegel, the only good (philosophically acceptable) kind of writing is that which respects the priority of self-present speech, and which therefore confines itself to a form of phonetic-alphabetical notation where writing must faithfully preserve and transcribe the character of oral discourse. Hence Derrida's reiterated question: *by what right*, or according to what self-evident law of reason, must writing be consigned to this strictly subservient role in relation to speech? For there exist, after all, a great many striking counter-examples, from the various forms of non-European pictographic or ideogrammatical writing which he discusses at length in *Of Grammatology*, to those systems of formalised notation that have often been proposed, by philosophers from Leibniz to Ferge, as a means of overcoming the vagueness and imprecision of natural lan-

Office for Metropolitan Architecture, Parc de la Villette, 1983-84, model

guage. It is against this background that Hegel's gesture of exclusion takes on its wider significance. For it brings out very clearly the link that exists between Western logocentric assumptions and a certain deep-laid phonocentric bias, an attitude which holds that writing is at best a poor substitute for speech, but one which can attain some measure of truth so long as it properly reproduces those speech-sounds that in turn give access to the realm of self-present thought.

Derrida's *Glas* is undoubtedly the text where this argument is presented to maximum effect through a writing – a practice of spatial and graphic inscription – which cannot be reduced to any order of philosophic concepts.[14] It has thus achieved something of a scandalous reputation as the *ne plus ultra* of philosophy's undoing at the hands of rhetoric or intertextual 'freeplay'. In fact this idea is demonstrably wide of the mark, since Derrida is here just as much concerned with issues in the province of post-Kantian (and especially Hegelian) philosophy. But they are addressed in a style – a typographical as well as a 'literary' style – whose effect is to provoke the greatest possible resistance among mainstream academic philosophers. The text is laid out in a running series of columns, commentaries and inset paragraphs, all of which the reader is supposed to take in by treating them on equal terms and not looking for some 'meta-language' or privileged voice of authorial truth. The two main sources are Hegel and Genet; on the one hand the philosopher of Absolute Reason, of the State, Christianity and the bourgeois family as embodiments of universal truth, on the other the homosexual thief-turned-writer whose aim was to tear those values apart by every means at his disposal.

At one level the effect of juxtaposing these utterly incongruous texts is to bring philosophy up against the limits of its own conceptual resources, to transgress all the margins and juridical border-lines that philosophy has established for the conduct of serious, responsible debate. Thus Hegel's dialectic is inscribed within a system of self-regulating concepts and values which ensure that truth is passed down through the channels of properly *authorised* thinking and teaching. This system connects in turn with the sexual division of labour where reason is exclusively a male prerogative, a power exercised by virtue of the husband's joint access to the domestic and civil spheres, while woman remains duty-bound to her role as wife, mother and family helpmeet. Derrida goes various ways around to deconstruct this covert gender-politics everywhere at work in the texts of Hegelian philosophy. He incorporates passages on love, marriage and the family from Hegel's letters and other biographical material; examines the way that his reading of Sophocles' *Antigone* turns upon this same dialectical overcoming of woman's interests in the name of male reason and political order. He then goes on to show, through a series of elaborately staged intertextual readings, how other philosophers (including Kant) have likewise managed to repress or to sublimate woman's voice while claiming to speak in the name of universal humanity and absolute reason. All this in counterpoint with the passages from Genet (chiefly *Our Lady of the Flowers* and *The Thief's Journal*) which supply not so much an ironic gloss as an adversary language which progressively invades and disfigures the discourse of Hegelian reason. Thus *Glas* opens up the domain of male dialectical thought to a series of complicating detours and aporias that cannot be subsumed by any logic of speculative reason.

There is so much going on at every stage in this extraordinary text that a brief account can really offer no more than a few suggested points of entry. One recurrent topos is the question of names, signatures and the way that such marks of authorial presence and origin can always be dissolved through what Derrida calls the 'disseminating' power of language, its capacity to graft them onto new contexts of meaning where they no longer function as 'proper' names but as signifying terms that generate all kinds of allusive cross-reference from text to text.[15] Another is the distinction between 'literal' and 'figurative' sense, a difference that philosophers have often been concerned to hold securely in place, but which nonetheless continues to vex and elude their best efforts of conceptual clarification. There is a whole running subtext of allusions (*via* Genet) to the so-called 'flowers' of rhetoric, the seductive tropology of metaphor and other such figures that exert their unsettling influence on the discourse of philosophic reason. And this goes along with Derrida's insistence on the stubborn *materiality* of language, the way that effects of meaning come about through chance collocations, unlooked-for homonyms and everything that holds out against reduction to a stable economy of words and concepts.

Hegelian logic thinks to overcome such resistance by assimilating language, history and thought to the terms of an all-embracing dialectic that moves ever onward and up through stages of repeated conflict and tension, to the point of an ultimate reconciliation in the name of Absolute Reason.[16] This movement involves a twofold process of subsuming and transcending whatever stands in its way, a process of conceptual 'raising' (*Aufhebung*) which also requires that reason should sublimate those previous stages on the path to enlightenment that reflected an as-yet imperfect grasp of the relation between thought, self-knowledge and reality. What Derrida asks us to read in his assemblage of intertextual echoes and allusions is the resistance that writing continues to offer in the face of this relentless totalising drive. Thus *Glas* draws attention to those episodes in Hegel's text where the narrative encounters something alien to the dominant (Graeco-Christian) tradition of idealised conceptual grasp. What is repressed at these moments is another history, one that Hegel attempts to bring under his grand teleological scheme of things, but which nonetheless continues to exert a steady disruptive pressure from the margins of his text.

Thus the progress of Hegelian dialectic is paralleled in his account of how Christianity (as revealed religious truth) supersedes and incorporates its Jewish source-texts, and again in his view of the bourgeois patriarchal family as the highpoint and natural, self-authorised foundation of present-day civil and socio-political order. 'What is consciousness', Derrida asks, 'if its ultimate power is achieved by the family?' And again, what is at stake in this repeated scenario of dialectical ascent or *Aufhebung* if one of its forms is the presumed overcoming of Jewish by Christian religion?

> To raise the pharisaic letter of the Jew would also be to constitute a symbolic language wherein the literal body lets itself be animated, aerated, roused, lifted up, benumbed by the spiritual intention. Now the Jew is incapable of this in his family, his politics, his religion, his rhetoric. If he became capable of it, he would no longer be Jewish. When he will become capable of it, he will have become Christian.[17]

This passage should make it clear that there is more to Derrida's 'wordplay' than a simple desire to take philosophy down a peg or two by exposing its arguments to the dislocating force of a Joycian paronomasia pushed to the giddy extreme. What he is broaching in *Glas* is the deconstruction not only of certain tenacious philosophical ideas, but also of the way those ideas have worked to reinforce the predominant values and assumptions of Western ethnocentric discourse.

Truth, Writing, Representation

It is now time to ask what relevance deconstruction might have to the visual arts and topics in the discourse of present-day aesthetic theory. One obvious point of connection is the fact that art criticism is a literary genre which has always been taken to exist at a certain remove from those objects it seeks to describe, elucidate or somehow comprehend by means of a written commentary. Thus Kant makes it clear that aesthetic philosophy – the discourse on art to which he contributes in the Third *Critique* – cannot in itself belong to the realm of aesthetic experience, since it has to do with determinate concepts, forms and modalities of argument which don't involve either that 'free play' of the faculties provoked by beautiful objects, or that higher 'supersensible' realm of ideas to which we gain access through the Kantian sublime. Having a theory of art is not at all the same thing as experiencing art in its essential difference from all concepts arrived at through a process of generalised aesthetic critique. Otherwise art would lose its most distinctive character, that 'purposiveness without purpose' which sets it apart from theoretical understanding, and which thus enables Kant to treat it *by analogy* as a privileged source of insight into the other faculties.

'I owe you the truth in painting': the words are those of Cézanne, in a letter that provides the starting-point for one of Derrida's recent texts. What could it be, this essential 'truth' in painting that the artist must somehow restore, render up or account for as a matter of ethical obligation? And again: 'must we take a painter literally, once he starts to speak?'[18] For such questions have more often been raised by critics and philosophers than by artists themselves, the latter having no great concern to theorise the truth-claims of their own practice. But what *competence* has philosophy to speak about the 'truth' in painting, given that this truth has always seemed to exist in a realm quite apart from the concepts and categories of philosophic discourse? And yet of course they have all had their say on this question, the philosophers from Plato to Kant, Hegel, Nietzsche, Heidegger and the modern analytical school. They have offered various judgements, positive or negative, on art's relationship to truth and its role in the conduct of a well-ordered society. They have laid down the limits of aesthetic understanding *vis-à-vis* science, theology, ethics, and of course philosophy itself, as the overarching discourse that assigns these 'faculties' each to its own proper place within the project of enlightened self-knowledge.

Some (like Plato) have devalued art as a poor substitute or, at worst, a dangerous rival in the quest for authentic, philosophical truth. Others (like Kant) have allowed it a large, even crucial role in their system of argument, but still made a point of *philosophically* delimiting its relevance to other topics of debate. In short, the entire history of thinking about art and its objects has been worked over by a series of 'philosophemes' – juridical concepts and categories – that seek to establish the essential priority of *logos* over *mythos*, reason over representation, concept over metaphor, the intelligible over the sensible, and ultimately truth over painting.

So the question has always been: what can art tell us, philosophically speaking, of its own relationship to Being and Truth? At a certain point – as with Nietzsche and Heidegger – the emphasis may shift to give art (music, poetry or painting) the privileged position, and then to demand that philosophy (or Western metaphysics) be measured against this deeper, more authentic source of wisdom. But we would be wrong to accept this shift at its own valuation, or to take their (Nietzsche's and Heidegger's) word for it that henceforth thinking will follow a different path. For as Derrida remarks, it has always been one of philosophy's most 'natural', spontaneous gestures to present itself as turning back toward some origin or authentic point of departure that has somehow been forgotten in the subsequent history of thought. Such, after all, was Plato's idea of truth as a kind of unveiling (*aletheia*), an inward revelation vouchsafed to the soul in a state of intellectual grace, as opposed to that other, less reputable kind that relied on *mimesis*, phenomenal cognition, or a certain correspondence between real-world objects and representations thereof. Quite simply, there is no philosophical discourse on, or of, art that would allow it to speak (as Heidegger wished) in a language of primordial truth uncorrupted by the various accretions of Western metaphysical thought. 'These questions are all taken from a determinate set. Determined according to history and system. The history would be that of philosophy within which the history of the philosophy of art would be marked off, in so far as it treats of art and of the history of art.' (*TP* 18) Any attempt to think the limits of this system – as Derrida proposes in *The Truth in Painting* – will have to reckon with philosophy's having always provided the script or staked out the conceptual ground in advance.

Of course one might think to escape this predicament by declaring that art has *nothing to do* with philosophy or theory; that aesthetics is and always has been a pointless, misconceived enterprise; and that therefore philosophers had much better leave art alone and attend to those other sorts of question (ethical or epistemological) where their efforts may be of some use. But there are three main objections to this line of argument. First, we can have no 'experience' of art that won't have been to some extent programmed by those ideas of form, content, meaning, value, etc, which make up the legacy of Western aesthetics. Second, it is only *within* that tradition – on terms provided by thinkers like Kant – that art has taken on the aspect of a pure, 'disinterested' play of the faculties defined by its essential non-involvement with issues of politics, theoretical understanding, and so forth. And the third objection, which follows from these, is that art will fall prey to the most naive, the most uncritical and mystified forms of aesthetic ideology unless we continue to examine its relation to history, politics and philosophy itself, as the discipline that has always presumed to articulate their various orders of truth-claim.

And so Derrida asks: 'on what conditions, even if it is possible, can one exceed, dismantle, or displace the heritage of the great philosophies of art which still dominate this whole problematic, above all those of Kant, Hegel, and, in another respect, Heidegger?' (*TP* 9). His essay 'Parergon' takes up this question of the supposed autonomy of art and its relation to the various discourses (criticism, aesthetics, art history) which seek to preserve that autonomy. Derrida's point – briefly stated – is that all such distinctions must finally break down; that there always operates (in the terms of his essay on Rousseau) a certain 'logic of supplementarity' whereby the founding notions of beauty, sublimity, artistic truth and aesthetic value themselves turn out to be constituted by a discourse which comes, so to speak, *from outside* and yet inhabits our every utterance on the name and nature of art. The 'parergon' is the frame, the marker of limits, that which establishes – or so we might suppose – an impermeable boundary between the artwork (*ergon*) and everything that belongs to its background, context, space of exhibition, *mise en scène* or whatever. And Kantian aesthetics is likewise a kind of 'parergonal' discourse in so far as it claims to deliver significant truths about art while respecting the imperative boundary- conditions that prevent it from invading the artwork's privileged domain. In short, the whole analytic of aesthetic judgement forever assumes that one can distinguish rigorously between the intrinsic and the extrinsic. Aesthetic judgement *must* properly bear upon intrinsic beauty, not on finery and surrounds. (*TP* 69)

But it soon becomes clear from Derrida's reading of Kant that such boundaries are not so easily fixed; that there is always a tendency for 'inessential' details (outworks, parerga, ornamental settings) to thrust themselves forward and upset the logic of Kant's argumentation. This effect is both visible in the various illustrations that Derrida provides (paintings, statues, monuments, buildings, etc.) and detectable in those passages from the Third *Critique* where Kant introduces metaphors of framing in an attempt to delimit the proper space of aesthetic representation. What these passages often betray is a moment of *undecidability*, an instance of some seemingly marginal detail (whether 'inside' or 'outside' the frame) that in fact could not possibly be detached or altered without crucially upsetting the whole composition. Examples of this include the kind of merely 'decorative' outwork that affects what we perceive as a painting's 'intrinsic' quality; the 'clothing' of statues that (according to Kant) both is and is not a part of their 'essential' form; and in architecture, certain kinds of pillar or column that might seem to serve a purely functional purpose, but which cannot in the end be excluded from the overall artistic impression. And so, as Derrida writes,

> When Kant replies to our question 'What is a frame?' by saying it's a *parergon*, a hybrid of outside and inside, but a hybrid which is not a mixture or a half-measure, an outside which is called to the inside of the inside in order to constitute it as an inside; and when he gives as examples of the *parergon*, alongside the frame, clothing and column, we ask to see, we say to ourselves that there are 'great difficulties' here, and that the choice of examples, and their association, is not self-evident. (*TP* 63)

For there is simply no deciding just what is 'intrinsic' to the artwork and what belongs either *to* or *outside* the frame. And this doubt extends to the discourse of aesthetic philosophy, a 'framing' discourse whose chief concern (at least since Kant) has been precisely to legitimise its own existence by fixing the boundary between art and other modes of knowledge, including – paradoxically – art history and theory.

One purpose of Derrida's essay is to demystify this notion of the aesthetic as a realm of purely disinterested values, one in which conflicts are laid to rest through the 'free play' of the harmonised faculties. Thus he goes on to examine the various oppositions (like that between 'pure' and 'adherent' beauty) which organise the Kantian discourse on art. In a subsequent chapter of *The Truth in Painting* ('Restitutions') Derrida pursues this argument by asking what is at stake – what particular *interests* of a socio-political nature – when an American art critic, Meyer Schapiro, takes issue with Heidegger over Van Gogh's painting *Old Shoes with Laces*.[19] The question is one of ownership, of who these shoes actually belonged to, with Heidegger asserting for his part that this must be a pair of peasant boots, bearing all the signs of an authentic existence lived out in proximity to the earth. Schapiro disagrees: these are city-dweller's shoes, most likely belonging to Van Gogh himself, and Heidegger's mistake can best be understood as a species of fantasy investment, a projection onto the painting of his own philosophical concerns. Thus Heidegger has 'annexed the shoes to his social landscape and hypercathected them with his "heavy pathos of the native and the countryman"' (*TP* 366). But then what of Schapiro, the disinterested scholar-critic, he whose only wish (or so it seems) is to see justice done, to restore these shoes to their rightful owner and clear up a case of mistaken attribution with certain rather sinister ideological overtones? At this point Derrida recounts a complicated story wherein Schapiro's attention is drawn to the Heidegger essay by a German Jewish *emigré* colleague at Columbia, Kurt Goldstein, who had been imprisoned by the Nazis in 1933 and then fled Germany to spend a year in Amsterdam before arriving in America. Might it not be that Schapiro's act of restitution has something to do with this 'personal prehistory', this chapter of events that involved him so directly and at so many levels? For Schapiro was himself an *emigré* intellectual, having taught at Columbia with Goldstein, experienced some of the same political upheavals and dedicated an essay ('The Still Life') to the memory of his ex-colleague.

What are we to make of such 'background' information, facts that would normally be treated – if at all – as possessing a merely anecdotal significance, with no bearing on questions of aesthetic or art historical interest? On the contrary, Derrida asserts: this history 'is far from being indifferent or extrinsic . . . or at least the extrinsic always

Vincent Van Gogh, *Old Shoes with Laces*, 1886, oil on canvas

intervenes, like the *parergon*, within the scene' (*TP* 367). For there is simply no way of drawing a firm, juridical line between that which pertains to the artwork itself and that which supervenes as a consequence of the interests, life-histories, projections or investments that are brought to the work by these two contending parties. I must now quote Derrida at length in order to convey just what is at stake in this struggle for truth over the Van Gogh painting:

[I]t all looks just as if Schapiro, from New York, was disputing possession of the shoes with Heidegger, was taking them back so as to restitute them, via Amsterdam and Paris (Van Gogh in Paris) to Van Gogh, but *at the same time* to Goldstein, who had drawn his attention to Heidegger's hijack. And Heidegger hangs onto them. And when both of them say, basically, 'I owe you the truth,' . . . they also say: I owe the shoes, I must return them to their rightful owner . . . to the peasant man or woman on the one side, to the city-dwelling painter and signatory of the painting on the other. But to whom in truth? And who is going to believe that this episode is merely a theoretical or philosophical dispute over the interpretation of a work or the Work of art? . . . Schapiro bitterly disputes possession of the shoes with Heidegger, with 'Professor Heidegger', who is seen then, all in all, to have tried to put them on his own feet, by peasant-proxy, to put them-*back* onto his man-of-the-soil feet, with the pathos of the 'call of the earth,' of the *Feldweg* or *Holzwege* which, in 1935-36, was not foreign to what drove Goldstein to undertake his long march toward New York, via Amsterdam. (*TP* 272-3)

Now of course it is possible to dismiss such writing as a species of elaborate whimsy, or a casting-around for anecdotal details which can only obstruct our better appreciation of the artwork itself. But this is to ignore Derrida's point: that the discourse on art is *always and inevitably* bound up with the interests that belong 'outside' the privileged domain of aesthetic understanding. Moreover that discourse has functioned at least since Kant as a pretext for imagining that art gives access to just such a realm of timeless, apolitical, disinterested meanings and values. It would then be the purpose – or at least one purpose – of a deconstructive reading to point up the covert interests and motives in play when critics and art historians lay claim to the authentic 'truth' in painting. And this should give pause to those opponents who repudiate deconstruction as a narrowly 'textualist' enterprise, a theory that reduces everything to writing and declares reality a world well lost. What emerges most forcefully from *The Truth in Painting* is Derrida's conviction that there *is not and cannot be* any discourse that attains this aesthetic ideal. One need only look to his other recent writings – especially *De l'esprit* (1987) – to understand how Derrida's relationship with Heidegger has always been marked by this insistent awareness of the socio-political interests that actuate the quest for authentic Being and Truth.[20]

So when Derrida affirms, notoriously, that there is 'nothing outside the text' (more exactly: 'no "outside" to the text'; *il n'y a pas de hors-texte*) his words should not be taken as evidence that deconstruction is some kind of transcendental idealism or last-ditch solipsist creed.[21] The sentence should rather be construed as arguing first that we can have no access to reality except through the categories, concepts and codes, the structures of representation that make such access possible (an argument advanced by philosophers from Kant to many in the present-day analytic school); and second – more controversially – that *writing*, rather than speech, is the best, most adequate or non-reductive means of making this condition intelligible. This is writing *not* in the restricted sense of phonetic-alphabetical marks on a page, but a generalised writing – *archi-écriture* – which in Derrida's usage comes to include all those systems of language, culture and representation that exceed the grasp of logocentric reason or the Western 'metaphysics of presence.' Philosophy has traditionally claimed to offer a truth that transcends all accidents of time and place, that exists in a realm of ideal, intuitive or absolute knowledge. The recourse to language (a necessary recourse) can be sanctioned so long as language adheres to the order of priorities that leads through phonetic-alphabetical writing to a speech that faithfully enounces the truths of inward, authentic understanding. In Plato, this doctrine goes along with a deep mistrust, not only of writing but of all those kindred activities (rhetoric, poetry, drama, painting and the other arts) which supposedly lead the foolish astray with their representation of false images and ideas. For it is Plato's belief that the 'real-world' objects of phenomenal perception are *not* in fact the ultimate reality; that we can only have genuine knowledge of them in so far as we aspire to a truly philosophical grasp of the forms, ideas or essences to which they stand as mere localised material embodiments. In which case – according to Plato's mimetic doctrine – the artist must be seen as a double deceiver, one who offers a mere simulacrum of that which already belongs to the realm of secondary representation.

Thus art shares with writing this bad attribute of placing the beholder/reader at the furthest possible remove from authentic knowledge. Just as writing is conceived as the 'sign of a sign' – a substitute for speech which in turn stands in for the living self-presence of thought – so art provides a kind of shadow-play reality for those lacking the wisdom or virtue to pursue philosophical truth. Hence Plato's famous metaphor of the cave (*Republic*, Book II), depicting us as creatures of the dark, imprisoned underground with our backs turned to the light of day, while before us is enacted a flickering show of delusive images thrown upon the wall of the cave by an artificial fire.[22] Such is the effect of both writing and mimetic representation: practices which lead us to substitute error for truth, and to give up the quest for that authentic wisdom that comes of inward self-knowledge. If there is indeed a 'good' kind of writing, then it must be what Plato metaphorically terms a 'writing in the soul,' a language anterior to every form of mere graphic inscription and one whose source is that power of living recollection (*anamnesis*) which enables us to learn afresh what in some mysterious sense we always already knew. At which point Derrida can ask once again the question he puts to Rousseau, Husserl and Saussure: namely, by what curious twist of logic writing can figure in its literal sense as the source of all error and delusion, while a massively generalised *metaphor* of writing turns out to be the source – the condition of possibility – for Plato's doctrine of knowledge.

Double Sessions: Derrida on Mallarmé and Adami

We can now begin to see how the effects of deconstruction might register not only in art criticism – as when Derrida addresses the issue between Heidegger and Schapiro – but also in the very practice of painting or architecture. For on Plato's account truth is itself a kind of *mimesis*, but one that evokes forms or ideas already present in the soul of the wise individual, and which therefore escapes the disfiguring detour through writing or other such poor substitutes. What Derrida conversely asks us to perceive is the effect of a ubiquitous writing (*archi-écriture*) which disrupts this idealised mimetic economy and envisages a wholly different relation between art, meaning and truth. Most revealing here is Derrida's essay 'The Double Session', where he takes two passages (from Plato's *Philebus* and a short prose-text by Mallarmé entitled 'Mimique'), and allows them to enter into a play of mutual interrogative exchange.[23] The Plato text has to do with painting, and argues that the only authentic (virtuous) form of *mimesis* is that whereby the artist seeks to reproduce those inward truths whose essence lies beyond mere sensory representation. But in Mallarmé this doctrine is exposed to a series of textual displacements, complications and swerves from origin which make it impossible to know for sure just what is being imitated, or which came first, the mimic performance that Mallarmé (apparently) witnessed and now recollects, or the writing that seems to invent that performance in the very act of transcribing it.

Derrida goes various ways around in making this point about the 'undecidable' order of priorities involved in every act of *mimesis*. To begin with, he attempts – and signally fails – to reconstruct a plausible sequence of events leading up to the production of Mallarmé's elusive script:

> The temporal and textual structure of 'the thing' (what shall we call it?) presents itself, for the time being, thus: a mimodrama 'takes place', as a gestural writing preceded by no booklet; a preface is planned and then written *after* the 'event' to precede a booklet written *after the fact*, reflecting the mimodrama rather than programming it.[24]

This confusion of temporal and logical sequence is reproduced in the structure of Mallarmé's text, where Derrida locates a repeated effect of doubling, self-division of 'supplementarity' which cannot be accounted for in terms of a Platonist (logocentric) doctrine of mimesis. As he says, 'there is no longer any model, and hence, no copy, and . . . this structure (which encompasses Plato's text, including his attempt to escape it) is no longer being referred back to any ontology.'[25] In part, this deconstruction takes the form of a patient, meticulous close-reading of Mallarmé's text, one that – as Derrida is at pains to point out – pays the maximum regard to its syntax, logic and structures of semantic entailment. But it also involves a form of irreducibly graphic representation, an insistence on the visual aspect of writing as a certain arrangement of marks on the page, material inscriptions which cannot be reduced to a logocentric order of meaning and truth. For it is Mallarmé's achievement, as poet and essayist alike, to have pressed the signifying potential of language to a point where it exceeds that restricted economy, and where writ-

ing acquires the kind of spatial quality possessed by various forms of hieroglyphic or ideogrammatical script. Thus his work can be seen to challenge the conventional (but deeply naturalised) order of priorities which insists on phonetic-alphabetical writing as the only kind that can possibly preserve the self-presence of authentic speech.

This is why Derrida prints the two texts (Plato and Mallarmé) on a single page, with 'Mimique' enframed by the *Philebus* as a kind of disruptive inset, a gloss on Plato's argument which throws all its ruling assumptions into doubt.

His point is not simply to appeal to some vague notion of 'intertextuality' which would treat philosophy as just one more kind of writing and reject all the protocols of logic and reason. Rather, it is to bring out the constitutive limits of any reading that ignores the visual (in this case typographical) aspect of the text, and takes it for granted that signs point back to a 'transcendental signified' – or ultimate meaning – ideally remote from the vagaries of mere literal inscription. The effect is to confront Plato's doctrine with a writing that cuts across conventional ideas of the difference between mimetic representation on the one hand and textual, written or alphabetic signs on the other. For it is a main point of Derrida's argument that these borderlines are always a potential site of conflict; that they are held in place by a classical distribution of meanings, values and mimetic assumptions that cannot be breached without a certain 'violence' which in turn may provoke all manner of hostile responses.

Hence the desire of philosophers like Plato and Kant to put a frame around the artwork, to delimit the space of aesthetic representation by declaring mimesis a unique, 'disinterested', unworldly kind of activity, one that should ideally have nothing to do with extraneous concerns like history, politics or writing. For Plato, this is the 'good' mimesis, that which aspires to a 'writing in the soul' somehow cut off from all grossly material inscriptions. For Kant, it is what makes the difference between 'pure' and 'adherent' beauty, or aesthetic experience in its true, disinterested form and the valuing of beautiful objects for some other, practical or non-aesthetic reason. So when Derrida questions this parergonal logic of exclusion – as by 'framing' the Mallarmé text within the passage from Plato's *Philebus*, but allowing the Mallarmé to invert this relation, to overrun its borders and exert a subtle deconstructive pressure on Plato's arguments and metaphors – the effect is

SOCRATES: And if he had someone with him, he would put what he said to himself into actual speech addressed to his companion, audibly uttering those same thoughts, so that what before we called opinion (δόξαν) has now become assertion (λόγος).—PROTARCHUS: Of course.—SOCRATES: Whereas if he is alone he continues thinking the same thing by himself, going on his way maybe for a considerable time with the thought in his mind.—PROTARCHUS: Undoubtedly.—SOCRATES: Well now, I wonder whether you share my view on these matters.—PROTARCHUS: What is it?—SOCRATES: It seems to me that at such times our soul is like a book (Δοκεῖ μοι τότε ἡμῶν ἡ ψυχὴ βιβλίῳ τινὶ προσεοικέναι).—PROTARCHUS: How so?—SOCRATES: It appears to me that the conjunction of memory with sensations, together with the feelings consequent upon memory and sensation, may be said as it were to write words in our souls (γράφειν ἡμῶν ἐν ταῖς ψυχαῖς τότε λόγους). And when this experience writes what is true, the result is that true opinion and true assertions spring up in us, while when the internal scribe that I have suggested writes what is false (ψευδῆ δ' ὅταν ὁ τοιοῦτος παρ' ἡμῖν γραμματεὺς γράψῃ), we get the opposite sort of opinions and assertions. —PROTARCHUS: That certainly seems to me right, and I approve of the way you put it—SOCRATES: Then please give your approval to the presence of a second artist (δημιουργὸν) in our souls at such a time.—PROTARCHUS: Who is that?—SOCRATES: A painter (Ζωγράφον) who comes after the writer and paints in the soul pictures of these assertions that we make.—PROTARCHUS: How do we make out that he in his turn acts, and when?—SOCRATES: When we have got those opinions and assertions clear of the act of sight ('ὄψεως) or other sense, and as it were see in ourselves pictures or images (εἰκόνας) of what we previously opined or asserted. That does happen with us, doesn't it?—PROTARCHUS: Indeed it does.—SOCRATES: Then are the pictures of true opinions and assertions true, and the pictures of false ones false?—PROTARCHUS: Unquestionably.—SOCRATES: Well, if we are right so far, here is one more point in this connection for us to consider.—PROTARCHUS: What is that?—SOCRATES: Does all this necessarily befall us in respect of the present (τῶν ὄντων) and the past (τῶν γεγονότων), but not in respect of the future (τῶν μελλόντων)?—PROTARCHUS: On the contrary, it applies equally to them all.—SOCRATES: We said previously, did we not, that pleasures and pains felt in the soul alone might precede those that come through the body? That must mean that we have anticipatory pleasures and anticipatory pains in regard to the future.—PROTARCHUS: Very true.—SOCRATES: Now do those writings and paintings (γράμματά τε καὶ ξωγραφήματα), which a while ago we assumed to occur within ourselves, apply to past and present only, and not to the future?—PROTARCHUS: Indeed they do.—SOCRATES: When you say 'indeed they do', do you mean that the last sort are all expectations concerned with what is to come, and that we are full of expectations all our life long?—PROTARCHUS: Undoubtedly.—SOCRATES: Well now, as a supplement to all we have said, here is a further question for you to answer.

MIMIQUE

Silence, sole luxury after rhymes, an orchestra only marking with its gold, its brushes with thought and dusk, the detail of its signification on a par with a stilled ode and which it is up to the poet, roused by a dare, to translate! the silence of an afternoon of music; I find it, with contentment, also, before the ever original reappearance of Pierrot or of the poignant and elegant mime Paul Margueritte.

Such is this PIERROT MURDERER OF HIS WIFE composed and set down by himself, a mute soliloquy that the phantom, white as a yet unwritten page, holds in both face and gesture at full length to his soul. A whirlwind of naive or new reasons emanates, which it would be pleasing to seize upon with security: the esthetics of the genre situated closer to principles than any! (no)thing in this region of caprice foiling the direct simplifying instinct... This — "The scene illustrates but the idea, not any actual action, in a hymen (out of which flows Dream), tainted with vice yet sacred, between desire and fulfillment, perpetration and remembrance: here anticipating, there recalling, in the future, in the past, *under the false appearance of a present*. That is how the Mime operates, whose act is confined to a perpetual allusion without breaking the ice or the mirror: he thus sets up a medium, a pure medium, of fiction." Less than a thousand lines, the role, the one that reads, will instantly comprehend the rules as if placed before the stageboards, their humble depository. Surprise, accompanying the artifice of a notation of sentiments by unproffered sentences — that, in the sole case, perhaps, with authenticity, between the sheets and the eye there reigns a silence still, the condition and delight of reading.

J. Derrida, *Dissemination*, Athelone Press, London / University of Chicago Press, 1981, p. 175

something more than a mild jolt to our post-Gutenberg habits of literate thought.

We can see how this lesson applies, so to speak, from the opposite direction in Derrida's essay on Valerio Adami (collected in *The Truth in Painting*). His 'texts' are a series of studies, sketches and drawings which incorporate elements of a 'literal' writing – letters, signatures, citations, passages from Derrida's *Glas* – but which also exist in a kind of undecidable suspension between mimesis and that other kind of writing that mimesis supposedly excludes. 'At the point of this text (general text, I'm not going to define it again in all the cog wheels or energies of its apparatus), the angular signature of Adami was waiting for me. A stupefying advance, and one made simultaneously on all fronts (historical, theoretical, formal, political etc.)' [*TP* 56] At one level these 'advances' have to do with Adami's use of certain highly-charged thematic material, including the signature of Walter Benjamin, the German-Jewish Marxist intellectual whose death as a fugitive from Nazi persecution, and whose cryptic meditations on the destiny of art in an age of mechanical reproduction, clearly have a bearing on Derrida's and Adami's work.[26] But there is also, beyond this, a 'parergonal' effect of breaching the frame between art and non-art – or mimesis and writing – which, according to Derrida, exerts its own pressure on the dominant categories of thought and representation. What he seeks to bring out in these sketches of Adami is something much akin to the deconstructive reading of Platonist metaphysics in 'The Double Session'. Just as, for Benjamin, 'the function of art is no longer grounded in a ritual but on another praxis: it has its foundation in politics,' so likewise in Adami the moment of production is captured in a writing that inscribes the contingencies of history, chance and event, and which cannot be absorbed within a classical doctrine of mimesis as revealed truth.

The following passage may help to explain just what it is in Adami's work that solicits Derrida's interest and lends itself to the purposes of a deconstructive reading.

An edgeless textuality destructures and reinscribes the metaphysical motif of the absolute referent, of the thing itself in its final instance: neither that formalist and nonfigurative scripturalism which would come to efface or deny the scene supporting it (a scene which is historical, theoretical, political etc.), nor a 'left-realism', the codified simplification or the politicist stereotype which would annul the scientific event, also squeezing out the layer of discourse, the thickness of culture, ideological efficacy. (*TP* 175)

This passage finds a parallel in Derrida's treatment of the issue between Plato and Mallarmé, the gesture whereby there opens up 'an internal division within mimesis', so that 'reference is discreetly but absolutely displaced in the workings of a certain syntax, whenever any writing both marks and goes back over its mark with an undecidable stroke.'[27] But we would be wrong to suppose – like so many of Derrida's critics on the left – that the result of this gesture is to isolate art and writing in a realm of endlessly multiplied textual reinscriptions that bear no relation to history or politics. On the contrary: it joins with Benjamin's stress on the need to 'politicise aesthetics,' to reject that traditional way of thinking about art whereby the object is invested with a timeless self-authenticating value, an 'aura' deriving from its privileged status as an *original*, not merely a copy, supplement or work of 'mechanical reproduction.'[28] This is what Derrida reads in Adami, and also what he finds subtly but powerfully at work in Mallarmé's re-writing of Platonist themes. For the alternative – as Benjamin argues – is a form of mystified thinking that has always tended to 'aestheticise politics', to treat art as a realm of transcendent meanings and values where politics can have no place.

The question is therefore one of borders or juridical limits, of the way that various discursive domains are marked off one from another, with art assigned its own proper place within the overall economy of knowledge and representation. It is also – and especially in Benjamin's case – a matter of political boundaries, those which can determine issues of life or death on the basis of a line arbitrarily drawn between nation-states. For Benjamin committed suicide at the frontier between France and Spain when the border-guards refused him permission to cross as a refugee from the occupying German forces. This event is not merely 'represented' in Adami's work but inscribed more forcefully through a series of mimetic displacements and internal 'framing' devices. Their effect is to require that the picture be *read* as a document, a kind of compacted textual archive, rather than scanned with an eye to its attributes of aesthetic form or technique. As Derrida writes:

Here by another frontier, like the Franco-Spanish frontier, above, under the gazeless vigilance of a sentry, Spanish or French, it matters little, the political

Valerio Adami, *Ritratto di Walter Benjamin*, 1973, oil on canvas

force is the same on both sides . . . On the one side the German Benjamin hunted by the Nazis and repulsed by the Occupation forces (above the frontier the colour will be close to grey-green), below it will be the red of a Benjamin (his head is caught in it) equally under surveillance, betrayed, repressed, like red Spain. Under his name the frontier traverses his head, strikes and cuts at the forehead level. (*TP* 178)

Such a reading does more than simply draw upon 'themes' in Benjamin's work by way of providing a context or historical background for Adami's cryptic design. It demands that we reject these normative ideas about form and content, meaning and style, qualities 'intrinsic' to the artwork and facts that may register, at most, as possessing some kind of anecdotal or documentary interest. For Benjamin's life-history is *written* here in such a manner as to make the picture unreadable except in terms of that material practice of aesthetic production which Benjamin was among the first to theorise.

Hieroglyph of a biography, of theory, of politics, allegory of the 'subject' – of Benjamin in Benjamin's sense and name – a narrative fresco in a projection speeded up to the limit of instantaneity, synopsis of a film in which all the metonymic fragments . . . hold as if in suspense an interrupted breaching force, the *gestus* of a blow seized by death. (*TP* 179)

It is this writing of events – this series of inscriptions literally *there on the page*, unlike Plato's metaphorical 'writing in the soul' – that enables us to read Adami's work in relation to Benjamin's materialist theses. And it is equally the function of aesthetic ideology, in its Platonist or more recent (post-Kantian) forms, to pre-empt such a reading by its insistence that art belongs to a wholly separate realm of mimesis or revealed truth.

Hence Derrida's particular concern with the Kantian doctrine of the faculties, the 'architectonic' wherein different orders of truth-claim (theoretical understanding, practical reason, aesthetic judgement) are each in turn summoned before a critical tribunal whose task is to establish their powers and limits.[29] For this system is closely bound up with a whole set of institutional rules and procedures which mark out – for instance – the division of intellectual labour between university departments, the distinction between 'pure' and 'applied' research, between reason in its critical and instrumental aspects, and so forth. In his recent work Derrida has laid increasing stress on the need for deconstruction to address these issues in the politics of know-ledge, and to show how the system ultimately rests on a series of deeply-entrenched hierarchical oppositions whose logic may yet be called in doubt by a deconstructive reading of its primary texts. At one level, therefore, this analysis proceeds through a deconstruction of the boundary-markers that constitute the various disciplines. For the modern university has been conceived since Kant as a place where these faculties can exist side by side, pursuing diffe-rent interests and advancing different truth-claims but each within the limits of its own special competence, so that no single discipline threatens to encroach on the others' domain.[30]

Thus the arts, or the 'humanities' in general, are thought of as inhabiting a realm of pure, 'disinterested' knowledge unaffected by the various workaday pressures and impera-tives that govern the conduct of their 'applied' (mainly scientific) partners. It is precisely here – in the notional ideal of a faculty exempt from all extraneous compulsions – that Kant locates philosophy's role as a discourse of critical reason. For there exists, he argues – or there ought to exist in any democratic state, any civil society or genuine, en-lightened university system – a forum where such issues can be raised without fear of 'external' intervention. In return for this privilege philosophy will observe certain self-imposed restraints on its own activity. That is to say, it will criticise beliefs and truth-claims only in so far as they fall within the province of enlightened (disinterested) reason, and not as regards their implementation in the public or socio-political sphere. And aesthetics once again plays a pivotal role in this Kantian discourse of the faculties since it offers an ideal or test-case example of detached, contem-plative knowledge.

What Derrida perceives in this parcelling-out of juridical domains is a mystification of philosophy's role, a refusal to acknowledge that in fact there is no longer (if indeed there ever was) any workable distinction between 'pure' and 'applied' research. 'From now on, so long as it has the means, a military budget can invest in anything at all, in view of deferred profits: "basic" scientific theory, the humanities, literary theory and philosophy.'[31] For strategic interests are now such that work in these disciplines might always pay off in terms of some conceivable war-game scenario or exercise in the rhetoric of deterrence. If decon-struction is to mount any serious challenge to this doctrine of the faculties, then it has to move outside departments of philosophy – or, for that matter, departments of comp-arative literature – and address itself to questions of a eemingly extraneous nature. Thus he writes:

> following the consistency of its logic, it [deconstruc-tion] attacks not only the internal edifice, both seman-tic and formal, of philosophemes, but also what one would be wrong to assign to it as its external housing, its extrinsic conditions of practice: the historical forms of its pedagogy, the social, economic or political struc-tures of this pedagogical institution. (*TP* 19)

This has been Derrida's main concern in his work at the Collège International de Philosophie in Paris, set up to encourage forms of interdisciplinary research that found no place within existing institutions. In his 'Fifty-Two Aphorisms for a Foreword' (1986) we are offered what amounts to a text in lieu of the charter, statutes or inaugu-ral document that would set out the aims and objectives for such an enterprise.[32] I shall end by looking briefly at the 'Aphorisms' and what they tell us about Derrida's ongoing work.

Against Post-modernism: the Politics of Deconstruction

This work has involved three closely related areas of re-search: philosophy, art criticism and the university – or teaching institutions in general – as sites where the question of power-knowledge comes most clearly into view. For it is through teaching that the various 'faculties' or disciplines retain their power to determine what shall *count* as genuine, authorised truth. And this scene of instruction is in turn closely linked with an 'architectonic' whose mean-ing extends – through a more than fortuitous pun – to the classrooms, the buildings and the whole institutional en-vironment within which those disciplines find their appro-priate place. Hence the need, as Derrida argues, for a questioning of the faculties that would also reflect on the material conditions of teaching practice. To suppose that these ought to be separate concerns – that the critique of philosophy and its founding assumptions can best be car-ried on without regard to such 'extraneous' matters – is yet another version of the logocentric drive to elevate truth above the mere contingencies of historical event. As Derrida writes:

> From its initial outline the Collège International de Philosophie was obliged to think its own architecture, or at least its relation to architecture. It had to be prepared to invent, and not only for its own sake, a

configuration of places which do not reproduce the philosophical topos (*topique*) which, quite rightly, was itself being interrogated or deconstructed. This topos reflects the models or reflects itself in them. The socio-academic structure, politico-pedagogical hierarchies, forms of community that preside over the organisation of places or in any case never let themselves be separated from them. (*Aphorisms*, No. 27)

The 'Aphorisms' make it clear that Derrida is not thinking in terms of some *analogy* or loosely metaphorical relation between philosophy, teaching and architecture. Rather, he wants us to see how these projects are all bound up with that enlightenment discourse of grounds, foundations, architectonics, 'constructive' argument and so forth whose structure has defined the very scope and limits of modern (post-Kantian) thought.[23] Hence his reluctance to describe future projects, or to lay down parameters for what the College might hope to achieve. 'To say that it does not have a project does not amount to denouncing its empiricism or its adventurism. In the same way an architecture without a project is engaged perhaps in a more thoughtful, more inventive, more propitious work.' (*Aphorisms*, No. 36)

This point is underlined by the aphoristic form of Derrida's text, a writing – like Nietzsche's – that deploys all the resources of style, paradox and self-reflective statement specifically *against* that 'monumental' discourse where philosophy and architecture find themselves most at home. There is, in short, 'no inhabitable place for the aphorism,' no means of assigning its proper role within a systematic edifice of concepts. Unless, that is, one thinks of the aphorism as a self-contained vehicle of truth, a lapidary statement whose very isolation from surrounding sentences ensures its privileged status. In this case Derrida writes,

> The aphorism resumes, reassembles everything in itself, like absolute knowledge. It no longer poses any questions. No interrogation/point of interrogation [*point d' interrogation*]: it is thus impossible to punctuate a discourse which is or which produces its own method and includes within itself all its preambles and vestibules. If architecture is dominated by the logos, then the character of the aphorism commands, it starts and diminishes: architectonic, archi-eschatology and archi-teleology. (*Aphorisms*, No. 44)

It is this recuperative power of philosophic language that Derrida no doubt has in mind when, alluding to the famous painting of Magritte, he declares that 'this is not an aphor-ism', and thus – by means of a self-reflexive paradox – prevents his own discourse from rejoining that hallowed tradition. What such writing seeks to achieve is a dislocating force, an energy of style that should not be confined to any project, system or 'architectonic'.

And indeed, one can look back to Derrida's earliest published texts – like the essays collected in *Writing And Difference* – and see how he has often engaged with philosophy at the point where it resorts to a certain metaphorics of building, edifice and form. Thus: 'the relief and design of structures appears more clearly when content, which is the living energy of meaning, is neutralised. Somewhat like the architecture of an uninhabited or deserted city, reduced to its skeleton by some catastrophe of nature or art. A city no longer inhabited, not simply left behind, but haunted by meaning and culture.'[34] That is to say, the self-understanding of philosophy has always involved this constitutive desire to bring meaning under the rule of concept, system and method, a desire which characteristically finds expression in architectural models and metaphors. Or rather – since Derrida pointedly avoids such terms – philosophy and architecture have both invested in a discourse whose founding oppositions (form *versus* content, spirit *versus* matter, the intelligible *versus* the sensible) cannot be brought into question without re-thinking that entire network of relations, priorities and structural ties which have governed their development to date. 'Contrary to appearances,' he writes:

> 'deconstruction' is not an architectural metaphor. The word ought and will have to name a thought of architecture, it must be a thought at work . . . Next, a deconstruction, as its name indicates, must from the start deconstruct the construction itself, its structural or constructivist motif, its schemes, its intuitions and its concepts, its rhetoric. But it deconstructs as well the strictly architectural construction, the philosophical construction of the concept of architecture. The concept is governed by the model both in the idea of the system in philosophy as well as in the theory, practice and teaching of architecture. (*Aphorisms*, No. 48)

One can therefore understand why Derrida should avoid all talk of 'projects' for the College, since this would imply that its work could after all be inscribed within that same familiar scene of instruction whose philosophic counterpart is Kant's doctrine of the faculties.

There is no room here for a detailed discussion of his

Réne Magritte, *This is not a Pipe*, 1929, oil on canvas

recent collaborative work with the architects Peter Eisenman and Bernard Tschumi. (Andrew Benjamin will in any case have more to say on this and related topics.) But it is worth remarking that Eisenman, for one, discovers not merely some suggestive points of contact but a profound identity of interests between Derrida's thinking and his own.[36] This has to do chiefly with those binary oppositions that have always permeated the discourse on and of architecture, but whose role in the dominant modernist paradigm is especially open to challenge. 'For architecture to enter a post-Hegelian condition, it must move away from the rigidity and value structure of these dialectic oppositions. For example the traditional opposition between structure and decoration, abstraction and figuration, figure and ground, form and function could be dissolved. Architecture could begin an exploration of the "between" within these categories.'[37] And it may be, as Eisenman suggests, that the only way to think such a radical transformation in our concepts and categories is by way of linguistic figuration itself, especially those tropes – like catachresis – that exert the most violently disruptive effect.

But it is equally important in this context to point out that deconstruction is *not* just a variant on familiar post-modernist themes. Hence Derrida's repeated denials (in *Of Grammatology* and elsewhere) that one could ever hope to break with the philosophic discourse of modernity – with logocentric reason or the Western 'metaphysics of presence' – simply by declaring an end to such talk and offering some alternative set of arguments. Only by working within that discourse and exposing its constitutive aporias or blind-spots can deconstruction effectively reveal what has hitherto been repressed. This is why it is wrong – a determinate misreading of Derrida's texts – to think that he has levelled the genre-distinction between 'philosophy' and 'literature', or shown that all concepts must finally come down to a play of uncontrolled linguistic figuration. Certainly there are texts – like the opening pages of his essay 'White Mythology' – where Derrida pursues this Nietzschian argument, showing how metaphor pervades the language of philosophy to a point where the difference between 'concept' and 'metaphor' becomes strictly undecidable:

By definition, then, there is no properly philosophical category to qualify a certain number of tropes that have conditioned the so-called 'fundamental', 'structuring', 'original' philosophical oppositions: they are

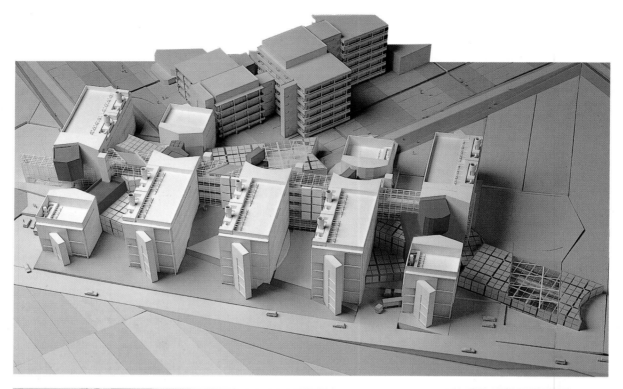

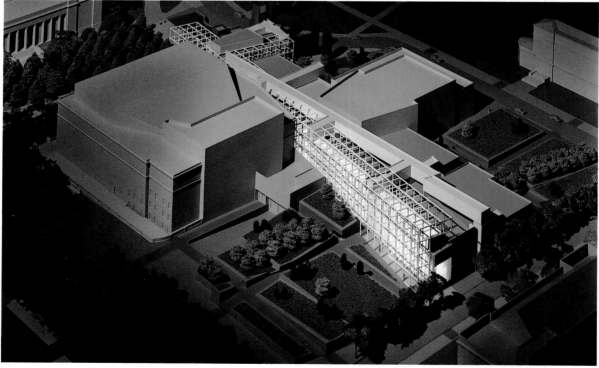

Above: Peter Eisenman, Biocenter for the University of Frankfurt, 1987-, model
Below: Peter Eisenman, Wexner Center for the Visual Arts, Ohio, 1985-, model

so many 'metaphors' that would constitute the rubrics of such a tropology, the words 'turn' or 'trope' or 'metaphor' being no exception to the rule.[38] But there is another side to this argument, one that is very often ignored by commentators – most of them literary theorists – who have a certain vested interest in thus demoting the privileged truth-claims of philosophy. For if all concepts are metaphors, and philosophy is in this sense just another kind of 'literary' writing, then equally it is the case that all our working notions of metaphor have been produced within the discourse of philosophic reason, through the various *definitions* of metaphor (and literature) produced by philosophers from Aristotle down. One cannot simply break with this entire prehistory, this structural genealogy of metaphor, any more than one can leap 'outside' the assumptions of Western logocentric discourse.

This is why Derrida insists that 'the concept of metaphor, along with all the predicates that permit its ordered extension and comprehension, is a philosopheme.'[39] That is to say, there is no avoiding the rule that philosophy will always, in some sense, have the last word, since even a radical anti-philosopher like Nietzsche – one who would treat every truth-claim as a species of sublimated metaphor or fiction – must perforce take issue with philosophy on ground of its own prior choosing. To ignore this endlessly repeated lesson is to opt for a kind of premature, self-deluding radicalism, one that can offer no argued resistance to the language it thinks to deconstruct. As Derrida says:

> To permit oneself to overlook this *vigil* of philosophy, one would have to posit that the sense aimed at through these figures is an essence rigorously independent of that which transports it, which is an already philosophical thesis, one might say philosophy's *unique thesis*, the thesis which constitutes the concept of metaphor, the opposition of the proper and the non-proper, of essence and accident, of intuition and discourse, of thought and language, of the intelligible and the sensible.[40]

This passage finds numerous echoes in Derrida's more recent texts, especially those that engage explicitly with topics in the history of modern (post-Kantian) critical thought. His point – briefly stated – is that deconstruction must at all costs 'keep faith' with that project, even where it works to problematise the arguments, the concepts or grounding assumptions upon which philosophy has rested its claims. For the 'vigil' of enlightenment can only be sustained by an attitude that questions received truths, that challenges the unthought axiomatics of Kantian thinking, but does so always through a critical encounter with the texts of that tradition. Otherwise it will amount to nothing more than a species of elaborate textual game, a handy technique for upstaging philosophy while leaving its arguments and assumptions untouched.

Hence the need – as I have argued – to distinguish deconstruction from those other, less circumspect modes of thought that proclaim their break with the 'modernist' paradigm as a *fait accompli*, an event whose signs are there to be read all around us. In philosophy, this event is most often identified with a wholesale rejection of enlightenment values, an attitude of downright scepticism toward all such 'totalising' projects or creeds.[41] From this it follows that post-modernism cannot take the form of a *critique*, an argued engagement with the modernist paradigm that sets out to challenge its grounding assumptions. For any such argument would have to be premised on a certain lingering 'enlightenment' ethos, a conviction not only that truth can be attained, but that the best way to reach it is by criticising those false beliefs, ideologies or pseudo-truths that have so far delayed its advent. We should therefore reject this whole bad legacy – whether Kantian, Hegelian, Marxist, or whatever – and acknowledge that there is no ultimate truth, no final 'meta-narrative' or standpoint of absolute reason from which to adjudicate the issue. Among literary critics there is a broadly similar consensus.[42] Post-modernism marks a decisive break with those old conventions (realist narrative, the omniscient author, fiction as a source of psychological or inward truth) that set the main terms of critical debate up to now. With their demise we can see what should always have been obvious, were it not for the hold of certain stubborn preconceptions about language, meaning and reality. That is to say, there is no truth, either inward or outward, that could validate one set of codes and conventions above another, or serve as the ultimate reference-point for a history of the novel – or of any other genre – conceived in terms of some grand teleology. All we have are the various narratives, language-games or fictive devices that in the end refer to nothing beyond their own transient power to make sense of an otherwise unknowable reality. And the same applies to philosophy, history and all those deluded meta-narrative discourses that once appeared set on the path of enlightenment and truth.

It is not hard to see how this post-modernist outlook fits in with a certain prevalent misreading of Derrida's texts. If one takes him to be arguing 1. that all concepts are really just disguised or sublimated metaphors, and 2. following from this, that philosophy is just another 'kind of writing' that refuses to acknowledge its own rhetorical or literary status, then indeed 'deconstruction' and 'post-modernism' would be more or less synonymous terms.[43] But this is not the case, as I hope will be apparent even from the brief account of his writings that I have been able to offer here. And the same caution should be exercised when attempting to locate 'deconstructionist' trends or motifs in the practice of contemporary painting, architecture and art-criticism. If the term has any use in this context, then it must be employed with a due sense of those *specific* arguments and strategies that set deconstruction firmly apart from any generalised 'post-modern condition'. Most important is the fact that post-modernism effectively collapses a whole series of distinctions that still play a vital (though problematic) role in Derrida's thinking. They include, as we have seen, such cardinal pairs as concept and metaphor, speech and writing, *logos* and *mimesis*, reason and rhetoric, art which remains 'inside' the frame of aesthetic representation and art which exceeds or transgresses the limits laid down by that framing discourse.

Obviously there is no question of providing some handy set of criteria which could then be applied from case to case in order to distinguish the two kinds of art. Any definition will be largely stipulative and involve some more or less dogmatic idea of what deconstruction supposedly 'is' or 'does'. It will also run the risk of falling back onto a language of intrinsic properties, values and aesthetic absolutes, a language that conspicuously fails to take the point of Derrida's arguments in 'The Parergon'. All the same there is a need for clarification, especially since the term 'post-modernism' is likewise subject to all manner of competing claims and counter-claims. What is at issue is the question whether or not these new styles of writing, painting and architecture have actually achieved that decisive break with the modernist paradigm envisaged by their various proponents. And if so, then the further question arises as to how this break should be seen in relation to present-day social and political realities. Is it – as the partisans would have us believe – an essentially liberating gesture, one that opens up new worlds of signifying practice by throwing off the burden of an outworn, restrictive,

monological discourse of truth? Or should we not see it rather as a last-ditch strategy of aesthetic evasion, a refusal to engage with those pressing contradictions that define what Fredric Jameson has called 'the cultural logic of late capitalism'?[44] In this case the 'post' in post-modernism would indicate not so much a movement *beyond* as a form of regressive or disabling historical amnesia, one that simply plays along with the styles, fashions and consumer demands of a thoroughly commodified culture.[45]

I think that this charge has some force when applied to post-modernist trends and ideas, but not when used – as critics like Charles Jencks have used it – as a stick to beat Derrida and deconstruction. Jencks appeals to the 'sociology of alienation' by way of explaining what strikes him as the emptiness, the nihilism and *anomie* of the whole deconstructionist enterprise. This has led, he writes,

> to the spectre of a world populated by 'other-directed' automata, what Harold Rosenberg has sarcastically termed 'Orgmen', that is, corporately conditioned and externally controlled ciphers who have lost their identity and history . . . And so we have the Deconstructionists' abhorrence of meaning and hierarchy, sentiments shared by Tschumi, Eisenman and Derrida, and their corresponding elevation of the Empty Man, the nomadic 'man without qualities' who can weave his way through all hierarchies showing them to be temporary and nonsensical.[46]

This description is so wide of the mark in Derrida's case that one hardly knows where to begin in unravelling the sources of confusion. But it is worth pointing out 1. that Jencks' comments would apply more aptly to post-modernist art and art theory, and 2. that they follow from his habit of conflating 'post-modernism' and 'deconstruction' as more or less synonymous terms. His failure to remark this distinction is perhaps one cause of the problems that Jencks encounters when attempting to provide a critical genealogy of present-day trends. The baroque profusion of descriptive terminology ('postmodern-historicist', 'latemodern', 'abstract deconstructivist', 'positive nihilist', etc.) suggests that some other, more crucial distinction is lacking in Jencks' account.[47] Philosophically, as I have argued, it is the difference between a counter-enlightenment outlook that annuls the very project of critical thought and a deconstructive attitude which calls that project into question without betraying its redemptive impulse.

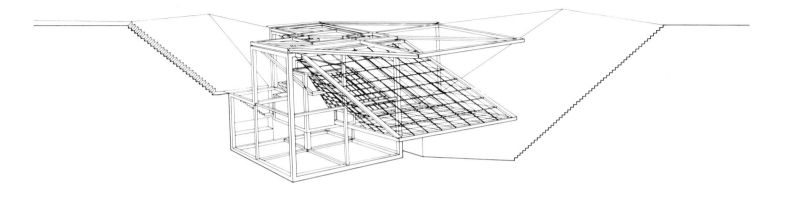

Peter Eisenman, House El even Odd, perspective diagram

Whether or not this distinction holds in the sphere of artistic production is an issue that the reader may judge for herself when comparing the various works reproduced in this volume. But I would suggest that any meaningful use of the phrase 'deconstructionist art' will involve at least some reference to the following characteristics. First, it will be seen how such work tends to juxtapose visual and textual elements, producing not so much a post-modernist collage of randomly associated styles and techniques as a critical, interrogative exchange between them. Second, this will have the effect of engaging the viewer/reader in an active decoding of the social constraints that are often concealed behind talk of aesthetic autonomy or form. (Thus Bernard Tschumi on his designs for the Parc de la Villette: 'the analysis of concepts in the most rigorous and internalised manner, but also their analysis from without, to question what these concepts and their history hide, as repression or dissimulation.')[48] And from this it follows, thirdly, that deconstruction maintains the kind of double-edged relation to modernist themes and techniques that enables such analysis to be carried forward without losing its point through the sheer multiplicity of styles on offer.

It is precisely in this critical attitude to modernism – what Derrida calls, in 'The Double Session', a 'displacement without reversal' of inherited concepts and categories –

that deconstruction exerts its power to unsettle existing forms of thought. Thus:

> any attempt to reverse mimetologism or escape it in one fell swoop by leaping out of it *with both feet* would only amount to an inevitable and immediate fall back into its system . . . one is back in the perception of the thing itself, the production of its presence, its truth, as idea, form, or matter.[49]

We might compare this with his essay on Adami, especially those passages that invoke Walter Benjamin and the question of art's ambivalent role in an age of mechanical reproduction. What we are given to read in these paintings, Derrida writes, is 'the active interpretation of x-rayed fragments, the epic stenography of a European unconscious . . . It is stratified, but simultaneously biographical, historical, economic, technical, political, poetical, theoretical'. (*TP* 175) And this can only come about in so far as criticism maintains itself on the problematic margin between painting and philosophy, a margin that cannot simply be erased without 'falling back' into various kinds of mystified aesthetic ideology. It is here that deconstruction offers not only an alternative but a *principled resistance* to that levelling of concepts and genre-distinctions envisaged by those who would leap 'with both feet' beyond the philosophic discourse of modernity.

Zaha Hadid, The Peak, Hong Kong, 1982-83, *Slabs*

Deconstruction and Art / The Art of Deconstruction

ANDREW BENJAMIN

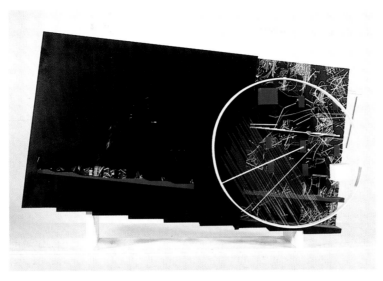

Daniel Libeskind, City Edge, Berlin, 1987, sectional model

Deconstruction Itself

Ce que la déconstruction n'est pas? mais tout!
Qu'est-ce que la déconstruction? mais rien!

The relationship between any philosophical movement and the actuality of a specific artistic practice is a difficult and complex one to describe, especially if the description is itself to be philosophical in orientation. In order to examine the relationship between deconstruction and art it is essential to start with deconstruction *itself*. The problem with deconstruction is what status is to be given or attributed to the *itself* and in what terms should the *itself* be understood.[1] What therefore is the *itself* that is being questioned? This may seem an odd beginning and yet it is one sanctioned by Derrida's own indication of what is involved in answering the question, what is deconstruction? In *Letter to a Japanese Friend* he makes the following important claim about any attempt to either define or translate the word 'deconstruction':

> To be very schematic I would say that the difficulty of defining and therefore also of translating the word 'deconstruction' stems from the fact that all the predicates, all the defining concepts, all the lexical significations, and even the syntactic articulations, which seem at one moment to lend themselves to this definition or to that translation, are also deconstructed and deconstructible, directly or otherwise, etc. And that goes for the word, the very unity of the word deconstruction, as for every word.[2]

The problem posed by the *itself* of deconstruction can be addressed by looking in some detail at this particular passage. Derrida's initial point is that any claim of the form 'deconstruction is X, Y or Z', lends itself to a subsequent deconstruction. In other words, it is not as though it is impossible to answer the question; indeed it is clear that a plethora of different responses can be offered. What must be recognised is that each one is neither exhaustive nor definitive. Furthermore any specific response is not immune from the activity that it seeks either to name or describe. This accounts for Derrida's further claim, made in a number of texts, that the word deconstruction can be replaced or substituted for other words; e.g. 'trace', 'différance', 'hymen', 'parergon'. Derrida's point is in fact larger than a simple anti-essentialism. His desire is to extend the argument from the initial claim about the word 'deconstruction' in order that it go on to cover words themselves.

Derrida's own arguments concerning the specificity of

deconstruction are to be interpreted as claims about philosophy, its history, and the language of its expression (and hence the problem of its uniqueness). These points become increasingly clear when it is realised that Derrida's claims concerning words and especially the word 'deconstruction' can be interpreted as a refusal to allow his own philosophical undertakings to be governed, controlled, perhaps even policed by the theory of naming that stems from Plato. It is precisely this theory which in its various forms and permutations has come to dominate the way names, words, definitions, etc., are understood.

It is not simply in the *Cratylus* that Plato is concerned with what a name names: it is, as is clear from the *Theaetetus*, a question that is central to any systematic philosophical investigation. Socrates brings this point to the fore in his question: 'do you suppose anyone has any understanding of the name of something, if he does not know what that thing is?' (147b2-3) Inherent in this question is the Platonic commitment to a conception of naming where the name names the essential being (*ousia*) of the thing in question. Such a conception of naming gives rise to a tradition that distinguishes between a surface level polysemy that lacks semantic regulation and an inner, unified original meaning. Here the problem of naming and of translation (translation and naming are for Derrida, and quite rightly, linked in an important way) concern the possible repetition of that inner content. It must be retained and repeated rather than transgressed.

Now one of the questions that dominates the Platonic dialogues aims at determining and naming the essence (*ousia*) of the particular subject of discussion; in other words its identity, as for example occurs in the *Hippias Major*. Socrates' question involves an important and fundamental distinction: 'he asked you not what is beautiful *(ti esti kalon)*, but what the beautiful is *(ho ti esti to kalon)*.'

The second type of question is appositely described by Dodds[3] in his commentary on the *Georgias* as a '*ti*-question'. Such questions are to be distinguished from '*poion*-questions' insofar as that latter are concerned with effects, or perhaps predicates, of that whose essence is being demanded by the initial '*ti*-question'. The importance of this distinction is that it opens up a particular mode of philosophical activity; one which allows for the possibility of separating universals and particulars and one where any answer to the question seeking the essence of the universal is always constrained by Plato's point that any answer to a

'*ti*-question' cannot involve merely citing an instance of that which is in question. More importantly it must involve the recognition that the essence must be a singular nature. It must be precisely this singular essence which is named in giving the answer to a '*ti*-question'. It is not surprising that this point is made by Plato in the *Cratylus* where he argues that for there to be such a thing as knowledge there could not be a series of conflicting answers to the questions 'what is knowledge?' It is rather that this question must yield an answer which gives the single and universal *ousia* of knowledge and it is only then that knowledge is itself possible. Plato's mode of questioning inaugurates a philosophical tradition that privileges Being over Becoming (the latter marked in the above by the term 'conflict') and hence inscribes Platonic questioning as a founding moment within the history of metaphysics.[4]

This digression indicates that the question 'what is deconstruction?', and Derrida's response that it is not 'one thing', involves a refusal to take over and carry on the tradition that dominates the history of philosophy. It is a tradition that is described by Derrida as the philosophy of presence; a conception of philosophy that is identified with the history of metaphysics. The resolute stand of deconstruction in relation to this tradition involves, in part, the promulgation of what Rodolphe Gasché has described as a 'system beyond Being'.[5] Given the problems involved in answering the question 'what is deconstruction?', any attempt to write on this subject necessitates a sensitivity to the place of deconstruction within the history of philosophy. What emerges as fundamental to the task of thinking as response to the question is a conception of language, translation, philosophy, etc. that will allow its refusal of the essential *(Wesen, essentia, ousia)* and the ensuing consequences of that refusal to find expression.

The refusal needs to be understood not as an avantguard gesture that dismisses the past – the history of metaphysics – but one which while maintaining that history does not allow it to dominate and thereby structure the presentation of philosophy itself. Linked to this is another fundamental element of deconstruction that emerges from Derrida's writings on both art and literature. What had hitherto been the case in the relationship between philosophy and art, and philosophy and literature, was a state-of-affairs in which philosophy dominated the literary text or work of art. Philosophy re-expressed them in its own terminology thereby denying the specificity of both the literary text and the work of art. Reciprocally this also involved an impoverishment of philosophy. Art, from within this perspective, is taken to be outside of philosophy and therefore its relationship to philosophy includes, if not ensnares it within, philosophical discourse. The work of art becomes an example. It exemplifies a philosophical position or claim. It is not difficult to see that this way of construing the relationship between philosophy and that which is other than philosophy (here art and literature) is articulated in terms of the opposition between the inside and the outside; an opposition to be deconstructed. The refusal of deconstruction to be entrapped within this opposition emerges from David Carrol's important observation that:

> Derrida's goal is to push against the limitations of theory and produce a form of critical discourse mobile enough to pass from art to theory and back again without terminating in either one. His work on art 'mobilises' both theory and art by *rethinking* each in terms of the frames that both separate them and link them together, that both block and permit passage or movement between them. (My emphasis.)[6]

The question that emerges from Carrol's description of deconstruction is how is this 'mobility' to be understood. Part of the answer is found in Carrol's additional claim that a significant and fundamental element of deconstruction involves a rethinking of the object. There is an important link between rethinking and naming; a link that provides for the possibility of rethinking naming.

Caution is needed here. Even in relation to the Platonic tradition, the *itself* of deconstruction eludes simple summation. A trap appears. Nonetheless it would seem that if the Platonic tradition can be encapsulated in terms of an opposition between a surface level polysemy and a unified essential meaning, then it is possible to interpret Derrida's claim that there is no single or essential answer to the question – what is deconstruction? – as involving the related claim that the plurality of different meanings amounted to a simple inversion of the Platonic heritage thus linking deconstruction to a more general argument for polysemy. The problem with drawing this conclusion is that it reduces deconstruction to a simple anti-essentialism that redescribed the locus of philosophical and literary investigation in terms of the capacity to identify and trace the consequences of multiple meanings or significations of the 'same' word. It would follow from this reductive interpre-

tation that deconstruction became no more than an unrestricted free play; in other words a type of anarchic semantic liberalism. Whilst this is often the way deconstruction is presented it is, nonetheless, a caricature that is far from the case. Indeed it is possible to go further and argue that the force of deconstruction is not found on the level of semantics. Deconstruction is not a theory of meaning. It does however involve claims about meaning. Indeed in his text *Signature, Event, Context*,[7] Derrida is concerned to present a theory of meaning where the conditions of possibility for meaning are to be found in iteration rather than contextualisation.

The consequence of the shift away from an understanding of deconstruction that construes it in semantic terms is that the purported *locus classicus* of deconstruction, the undecidable, can no longer be thought in semantic terms. To say of a word – as for example Derrida has done of 'pharmakon' – that it is undecidable, that its twofold meaning of *poison* and *cure* are always at play within any specific semantic determination, is not just to make a semantic claim. Indeed as Irene Harvey has argued there is already a link between this semantic 'duplicity' and translation. Her claim is that:

> The duplicity cannot be tolerated within a notion of translation based on the unity of a central signified.[8]

This point needs to be connected to the one made by John Llewelyn in his initial discussion of Derrida's, Mallarmé's and Hegel's attachment to what in general can be called undecidable terms. His point is that:

> What interests them primarily is rather that from which such words arise, that of which they are symptomatic.[9]

The question that arises from Llewelyn's point is what are these 'thats'? They are clearly pre-semantic. The shift away from a 'central signified' to what Llewelyn has identified is to focus attention on both the conditions of possibility for meaning, as well as the logocentric tradition in philosophy. Fundamental to logocentrism will be the refusal of undecidability. In its place will be unity of the signature, the name, the text, the translation, etc.

These points can be taken a step further by looking at one of Derrida's claims concerning the translation of the words 'he war' from James Joyce's *Finnegans Wake*. Of these two words Derrida says the following:

> *He war* calls translation, commands and forbids at the time the transposition into another language. Change

me – into yourself – and above all do not touch me, read and do not read, say and do not say other that what I have said and which will have been: in two words *who was* (qui fut). Alliance and double bind.[10]

The double bind which marks translation echoes Derrida's treatment of the signature in *Signéponge*. In both instances what is at stake is not the transgression of the laws of logic, nor a claim about the overdetermined nature of words. The point at play concerns the conditions of possibility for translation itself. Using the formulation Derrida provides in *Signéponge*[11] it can be argued that the law producing and prohibiting translation, and which produces the double bind, does not take place within semantics in any strict sense. The contradictory imperatives 'say and do not say what I have said' do not amount to the advancement or promulgation of a programme for translation; indeed these imperatives are not programmatic. A translator cannot follow them. And yet they gesture towards translation's conditions of existence. They are imperatives which, in the act of translation, come to be followed. They have no place in a manual listing translation procedures and possible equivalences. Their contradictory form further indicates why any translation of deconstruction, and thus any attempt to say what it is will always be marked by the necessity indicated by the interrelationship of 'alliance and double-bind'. At play here is the pre-determinate and hence the pre-semantic.

The 'pre' marking both the determinate and the semantic is intended to open up the possibility of thinking – of rethinking – translation, philosophy, naming, etc., independently of what Harvey called the 'unity of a central signified'. By extension, of course, such a conception of unity also incorporates the Platonic theory of naming and the conception of the word inscribed within it. It is within the terms set by the 'pre' that it is possible to return to deconstruction itself. The 'itself' cannot be thought of as a unity. Nor simply on the other hand is it an open ended plurality. Deconstruction is the attempt to think the relationship between the two. It is furthermore implicated in trying to determine how it is that what it deconstructs has come to be.

When Derrida argues that deconstruction is always already taking place what is at play in this claim is at the very least twofold. The first element necessitates the recognition that any text usually involves the presentation of unity and is thereby able to be deconstructed. Secondly the possibility of deconstruction is a consequence inscribed and implicit within that which sustains the impossibility of unity to dominate the text. The practice of deconstruction continually oscillates between these two poles. In addition they allow – as will be argued further on – for a distinction to be drawn between those works that attempt to exclude undecidability, etc., and in so doing attempt to inscribe themselves within the practice of unity, and those works which in recognising the dominance of what Derrida has recently called 'conceptual pairs' (e.g. inside/outside), articulate an affirmative literary, philosophical or artistic practice. It is not by chance (though the role of chance can never be excluded) that he uses the term 'affirmative' in discussions of *Glas*, de Man, Tschumi, Laporte.[12]

Fundamental to the affirmative is that it eludes the attempt by a logocentric philosophy – a philosophy of unity – to dominate it. Such a philosophy is in a very straight forward sense not equal to the task. The further consequence of this is that if deconstruction is always already taking place then this allows for affirmative readings, ones which can take place even if they are not sanctioned by the text/painting in question. An example here would be Derrida's 'double reading' of Heidegger. It is a reading that is precluded on one level by the Heideggerian texts – by the theory of reading and interpretation suggested by Heidegger – and yet because a redemptive reading is possible the importance of Heidegger for deconstruction can, *malgré tout*, be read. On a more general level this means that the relationship between such works and the activity of deconstruction must be one where, as David Carrol has noted, the movement between text, painting and philosophy provides a space where they can be rethought in terms of their separation and combination. Such a rethinking however does not aim to offer either the truth of painting or a philosophy of truth.

It is only by tracing Derrida's texts that are specifically concerned with an analysis of particular paintings, in addition to his recent work on architecture, that it will be possible to outline further the consequences of the double bind of naming and translation inscribed within the question – what is deconstruction?

Deconstruction and the Architecture of Affirmation

Derrida has insisted that despite appearances to the contrary deconstruction is not an architectural metaphor. Indeed deconstruction is not any type of metaphor. Derrida

Günter Behnisch, Hysolar Institute Building, University of Stuttgart, 1987

has linked deconstruction and architecture in a number of different contexts. In his work on Paul de Man and during an intriguing and important attempt to formulate the relationship – the differences and similarities – between their philosophical and literary critical endeavours, Derrida described deconstruction as that which:

> attacks the systemic (architectonic) constructionist account of what is brought together, of assembly.[13]

In the aphorisms which serve as an introduction to a collection of recent papers on the relationship between philosophy and architecture Derrida delimits the interconnection between deconstruction and architecture in the following way:

> To deconstruct the artefact named 'architecture', is perhaps to start to think it as an artefact, to rethink the artefacture from it, and the technique, therefore, in this point where it remains [reste] uninhabitable.[14]

The relationship between deconstruction, the architectonic and architecture takes place within a specific philosophical practice and philosophical thinking. A fundamental element of both is the refusal to allow either any conventional and thereby 'naturalising'[15] conception of either philosophy or architecture to dominate or provide the end – or home – for such an investigation. In relation to architecture this can begin with the attempt to break the automatic link between architecture and habitation. In regards to philosophy it would involve calling into question the distinction between theory and practice that positions the architectural edifice, or in broader terms, works of art, as an enactment of a particular theoretical/philosophical discourse. It is exactly this point that has recently been made by the architect Bernard Tschumi:

> It is above all the historical split between architecture and its theory that is eroded by the principles of deconstruction.[16]

There is a further and important consequence of the deconstruction of the opposition between theory and practice. Fundamental to such an opposition is a conception of the work – the putting to work of theory – as the enactment or exemplification of a theory or philosophical premise. If this opposition is allowed to dominate, then the inevitable result is that the relationship between work and theory comes to be expressed in teleological terms. The programmatic relationship between theory and practice identifies and thereby positions the practice as the unproblematic goal of theory. The deconstruction of the opposition theory/practice is therefore, and at the same time, a deconstruction of teleology. The deconstruction of one involves the deconstruction of the other. Teleology, theory and practice are interarticulated. If the opposition between theory and practice can no longer be said to provide the means or language by which to express the relationship between deconstruction and architecture, then a new approach needs to be found.

This problem can best be addressed in terms of the distinction already established between a thinking that takes place in terms of 'conceptual pairs' and to that extent governed by logocentrism, and a rethinking that recognises what could almost be described as the reality of deconstruction. (Deconstruction involves, while not being reducible to, a form of realism). It is in terms of this distinction that Derrida's work on Tschumi and Eisenman, as well as their own writings, can be situated. Derrida has tried to specify the relationship between architecture and deconstruction in the following terms:

> Architectural thinking can only be deconstructive in the following sense; as an attempt to visualise that which established the authority of the architectural concatenation in philosophy.[17]

Prior to commenting on this passage it is essential to note Derrida's emphasis on thinking. It is by emphasising thought as a mode of activity that the opposition between theory and practice is displaced and as such can no longer be assumed to structure the relationship between philosophy and that which is located (or locates itself) outside of philosophy.

Now, the question that must be answered is, what is a deconstructive architectural thinking? The first element involved in answering it is to specify what is at play in the 'architectural concatenation in philosophy.' There are many ways of doing this. In sum what is at stake in any answer is the architectonic that sustains philosophy (Hegel), that is deployed within philosophy (Wittgenstein) or through which philosophy comes to be expressed (Kant). Examples are to be found throughout the history of philosophy. (Indeed they are, perhaps, an intregral part of the dominant tradition within the history of philosophy). Included amongst them is Descartes' use of what could be called an architectural metaphor to present his conception of how to envisage a radical new beginning in philosophy.[18]

If, however, attention is paid to Descartes' elaborate use of the language of architects and builders, it then becomes clear that even though he wants to create the conditions for a complete break within the history of philosophy and thereby to start anew, his own employment of the architectural renders this impossible. Architecture undermines his desire. What is retained within the Cartesian desire for the absolutely new, what marks its continuity with what preceded is precisely the failure to rethink the 'architectural concatenation' within philosophy. It is not as though the new is housed in the old. Descartes' architectural metaphor betrays a failure to question. Descartes is working with the assumption that the language of philosophy – its metaphorics and the premises of its metaphorics – do not need to be questioned. The result of this is that while deploying the language of architecture to express the new, Descartes has repeated the architectural within philosophy and has thereby repeated that which is dominant within the history of philosophy. The Cartesian repetition is, in Derridian terms, a restriction of thinking. Descartes thought he was taking philosophy beyond a certain limit. In the end he was merely reidentifying the boundary by repeating it. The failure of Descartes to realise the desire for the absolutely new via the use of architectural language brings to the fore, once again, the question of what is a deconstructive, rather than a repetitive, thinking within architecture?

As is the case with all real questions an answer can only be gestured at. The work is, as yet, far from complete. It would, of course, be precisely in relation to this question that a deconstructive reading of Heidegger's *Building, Dwelling, Thinking* will become an undertaking of considerable importance. A fundamental part of Heidegger's own intention is the attempt 'to think about dwelling and building.' Heidegger's approach is situated within his general concern with the question of Being. This is clear from his description of his task:

> This thinking about building does not presume to discover architectural ideas, let alone give rules for building. This venture in thought does not view building as an art or as a technique of construction; rather, it traces building back into the domain to which everything that is belongs.[19]

Whatever limitation can be attached to Heidegger's way of proceeding its importance lies in the centrality it gives to a philosophical thinking. This leads to a consideration of Being and of the way dwelling 'is the basic character of Being.' The limit of Heidegger is the limit emerging from that which here sustains dwelling, namely Being.

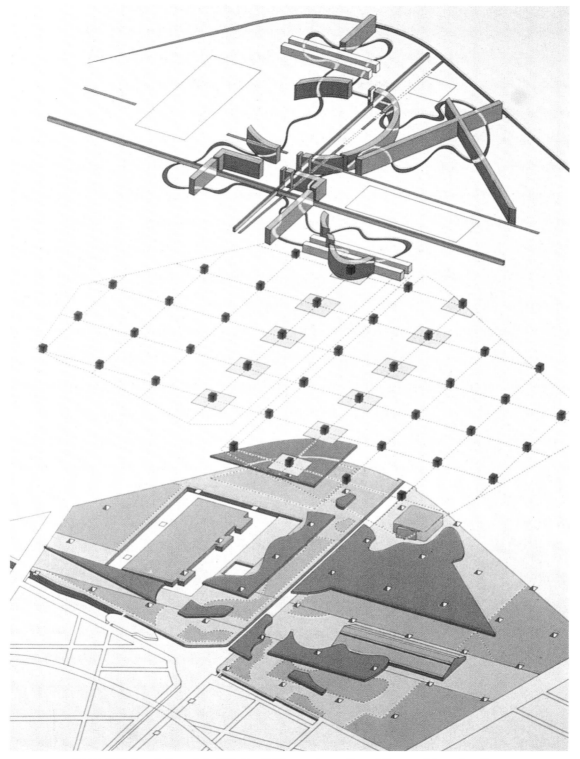

Bernard Tschumi, Parc de la Villette, 1985, superimpostion of lines, points and surfaces

Hiromi Fujii, Ushimado International Arts Festival Centre, 1985, main entrance

The path followed by Derrida differs. The investigation of architectural thinking points to a rethinking that is necessarily futural and to that extent disruptive; a rethinking taking place within philosophy and architecture. The connection between the futural and the disruptive joined as it is to a dis-placement of teleology and hence the absences of prediction figure, for example, within Hiromi Fujii's descriptions of his transformations and metamorphoses of an Edo store house:

> The repeated metamorphoses produce a 'balcony' space, yet, through these transformations we can no longer say with certainty what this space is. If our world is built up through the accretion of everyday experience and thereby becomes meaningful, then this can be said to be a deconstructed space that has escaped the confines of our world.[20]

Fujii's rethinking can be situated within a wider, more dispersed field of activity which is itself articulated in terms of the plurality of possibilities provided by the link between the futural and disruptive. On a general level this link further underlines the extent to which deconstruction does not give rise to, let alone permit, a teleological programme for its own enactment; one where the results were known in advance.

Deconstruction provides the frame in which it is possible to establish a distance from what has hitherto dominated architectural thinking. Deconstruction is however not framed by its own distance from domination. Both these last points emerge with great clarity in relation to the interconnection between humanism and habitation. In a recent discussion Bernard Tschumi described his work not as post-modern but as post-humanist. In so doing he provided it with a critical edge. An edge which cuts, leaving the mark of the political within architecture:

> It might be worthwhile . . . to abandon any notion of post-modern architecture in favour of a post-humanist architecture, one that would stress not only the dispersion of the subject and the force of social regulation, but also the effect of such decentering on the entire notion of a unified, coherent architectural form.[21]

Tschumi goes on to describe his work as involving an attempt to 'unsettle' and thereby to disturb. Is such an architecture habitable? The virtue of posing this question is that it forces attention not necessarily on what is to count as habitable but whether habitation is the *telos* or goal of architecture. Can architecture both disturb and unsettle at the same time as house and settle? Stemming from this

Peter Eisenman, House Six, 1976, axonometrics

formulation is the possibility – if not the need – to formulate a temporality of paradox. These problems and questions are addressed by what Peter Eisenman has called 'dislocation'. Dislocation in turn will provide a way of understanding the presence of habitation within architecture; the trait of habitation. In addition it will introduce via the trait the possibility of maintaining what Derrida has described as an affirmative architecture.

In the *House of Cards*[22] Eisenman is concerned to present a series of drawings and photographs of some of his recent projects and to accompany these with a series of texts, but at no time to specify in advance the relationship between all the elements. The book is indeed a house of cards. Eisenman has contributed an essay entitled 'Misreading' to the volume. (It contains additional material by Rosalind Krauss and Manfredo Tafuri.) Eisenman's text takes place around and is to be located in terms of what he calls 'dislocating', itself a form of misreading. Eisenman's subversion of expectations, projections, desires, etc., is meticulous. The reader is kept waiting and wanting only then to have them turned into ends without end. Paradox is central to dislocating:

Even as any architecture shelters, functions and conveys aesthetic meaning, a dislocating architecture must struggle against celebrating, or symbolising these activities; it must dislocate its own meaning. Dislocation involves shifting but not obliterating the boundaries of meaning, and since meaning necessarily implies absence through the absent referent, then a dislocating architecture must be at once presence and absence.[23]

Attention needs to be paid to dislocating.

Eisenman is not suggesting that architecture need no longer shelter or that it should cease to house. If this were the case then the logic of obliteration would have prevailed over that of dislocation. Architecture must however shelter and yet sheltering should not be coextensive with the edifice itself. This lack of coextensivity is the shift that marks a movement of the boundary of meaning. The architectural concatenation – here within architecture itself – is thus rethought. This gives rise to an intriguing point of comparison between Eisenman and Descartes. Descartes' desire for the new involved a repetition of the architectonic within philosophy. It remained unquestioned and hence it was repeated[24] within what Descartes thought was a complete and radical departure. The trait of metaphysics marked Descartes' philosophical innovation.

Eisenman is both more cautious and radical. On the one hand there is the recognition within his work that the architectural concatenation cannot be repeated within the terms set by its own repetition. Establishing the break that limits metaphysical repetition means that the link between architecture and shelter is called into question, and yet on the other hand architecture must house. The paradox that is central to his understanding of dislocation entails that there can be no absolute departure from the history of metaphysics, from the history of architecture. It is rather that architecture can no longer allow itself to be policed and controlled by that history. What has been handed down must nonetheless be housed and maintained, but it can no longer provide the explanation and *raison d'être* of architecture itself. The taking over and handing on of tradition cannot but repeat the architectural concatenation, while allowing it to remain unthought. No matter how resolute the taking over of tradition may be what remains forgotten is the architectonic of repetition itself. In sum Eisenman is suggesting a repeating and maintaining in which the metaphysical determinations of what has been repeated are dis–located and no longer function as the defining characteristic of the edifice itself.

The same type of argument can be used in relation to philosophy itself. (Remembering, of course, the problem of the 'itself'). The similarity lies in developing ways of understanding the future, and hence of a non-repetitive repetition within philosophy. Prior to taking up Derrida's discussion of 'maintaining' it is worth pursuing dislocation in its concrete form. This is not the same thing as the concretisation of dislocation. Dislocation involves, as will be seen, thinking. A futural thinking that cannot be – because it does not lend itself to be – automatically inscribed or expressed within teleology.

In *House of Cards* Eisenman described *House VI* as containing pillars and columns within the dining area which, in a conventional sense, 'disrupt' and 'intrude'. Interpreting them as merely playing the role of irritants is to accept the cohabitation of architecture and shelter as that which provides the basis and ground of interpretation. Once again such an acceptance would forget repetition. In moving beyond this constellation the columns – in fore-going metaphysical repetition – come to support the 'un-predictable'. They lend themselves to a different interpretation. Here difference is not just the possibility of a

different interpretation, rather it is the mark of the refusal to take over what Derrida has called a 'nihilistic repetition'. Difference has thus become the refusal of nihilism. Eisenman notes that the columns:

> have according to occupants of the house changed the dining experience in a real and more importantly unpredictable fashion.[25]

The relationship between the columns and the inhabitants cannot be expressed in terms of function of habitation (nor even in terms of the negation of that function). What is at play here is a relationship the consequences of which could not be determined in advance and thus were not in any sense the result of applying a method. Eisenman intended to dis-place intentionality:

> The design process of this house . . . intended to move the act of architecture from the complacent relationship with the metaphysic of architecture by reactivating its capacity to dislocate, thereby extending the search into the possibilities of occupable form.[26]

While an interpretation that reduces this adventure to a simple deviation or departure from a norm is always possible, Eisenman's intention is to allow for the unintended, in the sense of giving a place to that which cannot be predicted; a search no longer dominated by teleology. Allowing for such a search while maintaining the dis-placement of teleology is the affirmative within architecture.

Affirmation for Derrida takes place within literature, within philosophy, within architecture, etc. Affirmation has no specific boundary. In *Ja, ou le faux-bond*,[27] Derrida described *Glas* as involving an 'affirmative' deconstruction of the opposition between the arbitrary and the motivated. Derrida's use of the term 'affirmative' in this instance is as a counter to the charge of nihilism that tends to stem from a conflation of deconstruction and destruction. It also allows for a way of understanding how breaking with the control of 'oppositions', 'conceptual pairs', the language and architecture of metaphysics, redeploys *within* what had hitherto been seen to dominate form *without*. As has already been suggested affirmation within deconstruction involves this redeployment. This is not the end of the process for there is an additional element of great importance, namely that what is redeployed is maintained within what Derrida has called 'a space of interruption'. It is in this space that architecture houses and shelters while at the same time calling attention to sheltering, housing. Architecture is no longer reducible to, or explicable in terms of, the telos or

Frank Gehry, Winton Guest House, 1983-86, view from south

end established for it. This process, within Tschumi's *folies*, is described by Derrida:

> Tschumi's 'first' concern will no longer be to organise space as a function or in view of economic, aesthetic, epiphanic, or techno-utilitarian norms. These norms will be taken into consideration, but they will find themselves subordinated and reinscribed in one place in a text and in a space that they no longer command in the final instance. By pushing architecture towards its limit, a place will be made for 'pleasure'; each *folie* will be destined for a given 'use', with its own cultural, ludic, pedagogical, scientific and philosophical finalities.[28]

'Reinscription' involves a rupture that maintains. In the act of displacing both norms and function the work is freed from the reduction they demand. It is no longer an exemplification.

There are at least two important philosophical and theoretical consequences of the impossibility of this reduction. The first arises from the fact that the majority of philosophical and theoretical discourses demand such a reduction. The work must be seen therefore as an exemplification. The viability of any theoretical claim, within the terms set by the dominant tradition in philosophy, is found in its ability to express – in advance – the present and the future of its own practice. The future becomes the site of a predicted enactment, it is teleologically determined. If deconstruction, if thinking and rethinking the 'architectural concatenation' in philosophy, if the erosion of the split between theory and practice, point in a futural direction, then it is one over which mastery can no longer be adequately asserted by the history of metaphysics. In no longer being housed by that history the architecture of affirmation comes to house it.

The second consequence is linked to the first. Here what is at stake is the result of the split between, on the one hand, deconstruction and architecture, and the language of interpretation on the other. Affirmation and the affirmative enact this split. However, deconstruction, as Derrida argues, is also, always already, taking place.[29] It should not be thought however that affirmation is only to be discussed in connection with the work of Eisenman, Tschumi and Fujii. Further developments within architecture (and within the possibility of rethinking and maintaining that has been occasioned by Derrida's writings) can also be traced in the work of OMA, Rem Koolhaas, Dan Libeskind,

Coop Himmelblau, Frank Gehry and Zaha Hadid. The challenge posed by their work, as well as that of Eisenman, Tschumi and Fujii, lies in the attempt to understand the relationship between interpretation and deconstruction. The difficulty in delimiting the specificity of deconstruction has already been noted, the problem now is to answer the related questions that stem from the other half of this relationship. What is interpretation? How is the way toward or around a painting, building, sculpture, object to be found, charted, etc? In order to give an answer – not *the* answer, because *the* answer does not exist – it is essential to turn to Derrida's discussion *around* Adami.

Writing about Adami

In *Passe Partout* Derrida describes the four sections of *The Truth in Painting* as writing 'around painting' [autour de la peinture]. One of these writings concerns drawings and paintings by the Italian artist Valerio Adami. Derrida describes this particular writing 'around' as an:

> attempt to decrypt or unseal the singular contract, the one that can link the phonic trait to the so-called *graphic* trait, even prior to the existence of the word (e.g., GL, or TR or +R). Invisible and inaudible, this contract follows other paths, through different point changes: it has to do with the letter and the proper name in painting, with narration, technical reproduction, ideology, the phoneme, the biographeme, and politics, among other things and still in *painting*. The opportunity will be given by *The Journey of the Drawing* by Valerio Adami.[30]

Repeated here is the itinerary of Derrida's own journey. It is one which, despite its complexity, will be followed.[31]

The first point to note in this 'description' – the first stop – is the 'attempt to decrypt'. This attempt gives rise to the question of what is the distinction between interpretation, as it is usually understood and what Derrida has called the 'attempt to decrypt'? The answer for Derrida lies in the crypt. The object of interpretation is given; it gives itself to the interpretive act. The object occupies a 'natural place'. This differentiates it from the crypt.

> The crypt is . . . not a natural place, but the prominent story [histoire] of an artifice, an architecture, an artefact of a place, included in an other but rigorously separated from it, isolated from the general space by partion, enclosures, enclave.[32]

While this may generalise the crypt[33] it does nonetheless indicate the difficulty in approaching the included separation. However, the crypt – the included enclosure – betrays any straightforward attempt to construe what is called interpretation in terms of a revelation; a lifting of the veil and thereby exposing the truth of a work. What emerges from the description of his task as an 'attempt to decrypt', which then comes to be linked to the crypt, is the refusal to allow interpretation/reading etc., to be dominated by and hence articulated in terms of mimesis. To decrypt is to refuse to see/envisage the object as mimetic (this of course despite its own self-conception). Unsealing 'the contract' between the phonic and the graphic – to decrypt it – involves on the one hand the refusal to understand the relationship in terms of a mimetic showing and hence of representation. On the other it reworks what is to be understood by the phonic and the graphic; speech and writing become rewritten. These two elements combine to yield the further consequence that interpretation will founder if it necessitates teleology, mimesis, representation, etc. Approaching the work of art has become complex, because the work of art has become a complex. Not the complex as opposed to the simple but the complex as the framing of heterogeneity. As always care is needed. It will, however, be necessary to return to the crypt.

Derrida begins *+R (Into the Bargin)* – the text written 'about' Adami – in a cautious manner. The opening steps impose the question of how to write/read/decrypt etc. This cautionary approach is reinforced, albeit with a change in mood, by his abrupt dismissal of a specific type of discourse on painting. (Though by extension this point will also be true in relation to the other 'ands', e.g. philosophy and literature, philosophy and sculpture.) He goes on:

> Any discourse on it, beside it or above, always strikes me as silly, both didactic and incantatory, programmed, worked by the compulsion of mastery, be it poetical or philosophical always, and the more so when it is pertinent, in the position of chitchat, unequal and unproductive in the sight of what, at a stroke [d'un trait], does without or goes beyond this language remaining heterogeneous to it or denying it any overview.[34]

What Derrida has isolated here is the discrepancy that exists between the painting as the site of heterogeneity, and discourse, which in its desire to master the painting or work of art must deny that heterogeneity. The relationship between discourse and art becomes 'unproductive' if dis-

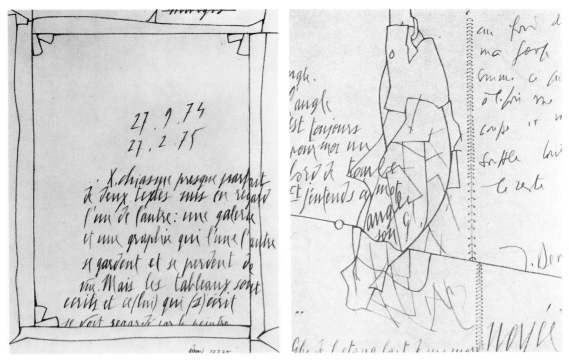

Valerio Adami, Studies for a Drawing after *Glas, 1975, pencil*

course aims to take over and express the painting. Painting 'goes beyond' the language of philosophy, poetry; or to be more precise it resists its langauge when that language aims at totality; totality as unity. How then is it possible to write about painting? Derrida's writing 'about' Adami, as has been suggested, offers an answer. One thread of this writing will be pursued.

Derrida writes 'about' Adami's 'fish drawing'. Derrida's first move is to break the power of the possessive – the 's' apostrophe – ridding it of its authorial mark. Derrida renames it; he baptises the drawing *Ich*. An arbitrary move though in part sanctioned by the drawing, resulting in the creation of a distance; a space marking survival. The drawing of the fish is part of a series of drawings undertaken by Adami and having the general name *Study for a Drawing after* Glas. Derrida, as the author of *Glas*, is already implicated in what is being written about. (Even though the content of this 'about' is far from clear).

Glas is concerned, amongst other things, with what Derrida has called the 'baptismal desire'. There, in the text, as a naming which can neither hold nor pin down. *Glas* deconstructs the power of the signature. Derrida's concern with signatures and proper names forms part of his larger philosophical trajectory. At stake, within the attempt to show how the unified and unitary 'I' becomes, within its own terms, an impossibility, is his attempt to deconstruct the Husserlian philosophical project as it pertains to the self or ego. The signature is articulated within a logic where in order that it function as regulative, as guarantor, as legislator etc. it must, at the same time, operate to deny that possibility. In writing about the poet Francis Ponge and the result of the implacement of Ponge's name within his own texts, Derrida notes the following:

> The law producing and prohibiting the signature . . . of the proper name, is that, by not letting the signature fall outside the text anymore, as an undersigned subscription and by inserting it into the body of the text, you monumentalise, institute, and erect it into a thing or a stony object. But in so doing you also lose the identity, the title of ownership over the text, you let it become a moment or part of a text, as a thing or a common noun.[35]

The fish painting contains both Adami's signature and also the signature of Derrida. Or to be more exact half the signature – 'J. Der' – the 'da' is missing. It is not there.

These may seem to be obscure points whose force resides

Daniel Libeskind, City Edge, Berlin, 1987, detail of site model A

and is limited to those texts bearing an internal signature. However to stop at this stage would be to miss the force of Derrida's point. The signature, and indeed this would also be the case with the self-portrait, seem to operate in terms of a presence which is fully present to itself. The 'I', or statements concerning the 'I' must be both unified and self-referential. It is precisely the impossibility of this that is made clear by Derrida's deconstruction of Husserl and the tradition of philosophical humanism. The authentic self-present 'I' is checked by the disseminated 'I'. This is the problem of the signature. John Llewelyn describes it thus:

> The author's signature, alienates as it identifies. Its owner is identified as, for example, the source of the intention of identifying himself by making his mark. But his mark is a chiasmus.[36]

The chiasmus – already itself there as a chiasmus of Derrida's babtism Ich – involves a curious logic.

A mark with the Greek letter χ [chi] is in Greek a chiazō, from which came chiasmos, which was an arrangement in cross form, from whence chiasmus, which in strict terms is the inversion in the second phrase of the order established in the first. Following Llewelyn's lead it can be argued that the move from mark to chiasmus is the move from the singular term to dissemination. In other words it is not a move at all but the announcement of what had always already been inscribed in language, names, etc., and which the logocentric desire for absolute self-presence had tried to still if not deny. The name therefore will always let itself be inverted, turned around and changed. That is the consequence of placing the name in the public domain. The chiasmus therefore marks the condition of naming itself. It should not be surprising that another Study for a Drawing after Glas presents the chiasmus. It is written within the frame itself. Derrida's own renaming of the Study as Ich not only presents the chiasmus of chiasmus, but presents the name as itself inscribed within dissemination. The Study has been doubly freed from Adami's 'authorisation'.

Derrida begins his translation of Ich by noting the writing that takes place within it. It functions as a mise en abyme. In other words they mark out, by inscribing within the frame, the activity that interpretation would seek to describe. Any attempt to establish an easy distinction between inside and outside is thereby checked. This inclusion within an enclosure is the crypt and yet it refuses representation and mimesis. In addition the possibility that interpretation is a secondary event occuring after the event being interpreted is cast into doubt. The posited primary event is as a consequence of the *mise en abyme* already inscribed within the event of interpretation prior to the act of interpretation. The usual temporal priority attributed to interpretation is thereby challenged. These are some of the results of Derrida's writing 'about' Adami. They are given the following more general expression by Geoff Bennington. He writes that for deconstruction:

> Reading is not performed by a subject set against the text as object; reading is imbricated in the text it reads.[37]

All these points seem to be exemplified (thus opening up the problematic of exemplification) by the content as well as the problems posed by the sentence:

> Je-marque seulement l'événement de Ich.

It comes to be translated as:

> I-marks only the event of the Ich.

The event is the *Ich*; the *Study* as baptised by Derrida. The *Je-marque* is the I that marks; (*Ich* is the translation into German of *je*). It is also the activity of marking, marked out in advance by Derrida. The dash between the *I* and the *mark*, emphasises its undecidability; the trace of one is always already there in the other. This is a state of affairs more prominent in the French since *marque* can be the first person singular of the present indicative, while in English *marks* cannot.

What is at play here however is the description, 'I-marks only the event of the Ich'. The event, as has been indicated, is one of great complexity. The importance of this is not the complexity itself but rather that it emphasises that 'I-marks' is a relationship that aims neither at domination, nor mastery, nor facile explication but a suggestive interplay in which philosophy and painting can take place as events of heterogeneity within and thus constituting an event of heterogeneity. Furthermore the event unfolds within an interpretive temporality that refuses the simple ordering of sequential continuity. It is precisely this emphasis on an initial heterogeneity that differentiates Derrida's work from Heidegger.[38]

Derrida starts by noting a number of threads within the frame. For example he notes that each letter and:

> especially *gl*, re-marks what is shown as what is said; slippery surface, [*surface glissante*] angular character, angled word, edge of tomb, hooded signature.[39]

Prior to returning to the *gl* it is essential to concentrate on the re-mark. What is it for something to re-mark, 'what is

shown as what is said'. The mark and the remark (equally the trait and the retrait) once again form an intergral part of Derrida's work. Gasché describes the re-mark as:

> that particular infrastructural feature that prohibits any diacritically constituted series of terms, concepts traces, or marks from ever closing upon itself. The impossibility of totalisation or self-closure . . . hinges on the existence of a certain nerve fold or angle on which . . . this impossibility is structurally based.[40]

The re-mark resists totality but not because of an 'infinite abundance of meaning' but, as Gasché indicates, because of the nature of the remark itself.

The *gl* provides a way of understanding the remark and in addition what is at stake in this particular writing 'about' painting. The *gl* can be traced in the left hand side of the *Study*. It occupies the top left hand side of a twice divided page. Before returning to the obvious question why *gl*?, some more ground needs to be covered. The *gl* sounds and is present. Derrida re-enacts the writing within the *Study*.

Mais gl? Son gl, Le son gl, le gl d'angle, son gl?

The *gl* is for Derrida neither a morpheme, nor does it take part in discourse. Furthermore it cannot be reduced wither to a 'spatial form' or to a 'logogram'. It cannot be represented or presented within the terms set by its own presentation. It figures within langauge and yet cannot be reduced to a mere element of its procedure. It figures within the frame and yet, again, cannot be reduced to a spatial form. The result of the *gl* – the re-mark *gl* – in *Ich* is, for Derrida that, 'Ich splits with one blow, like the fish both language and the picture.'

The fact that what Derrida calls, 'this fishing picture', is, after all, a *Study for a drawing after* Glas allows Derrida to pose the question of illustration and hence representation. And yet for Derrida *Ich* 'develops a scene' that is not a repetition of a scene from *Glas*, The major reason why this is the case is that, 'Ich performs its own operation.' Via the hook lifting the fish – entrapping it between life and death – Adami brings into play another scene of interpretation. It is one that is immediately recognised by Derrida and is to be seen in Adami's painting *Freud on Vacation*. (The hand beneath the head, holding hooks would lend itself, in another language – and as a translation – to a reading in 'h'.) The Freudian other scene is the unconscious. Here it is brought into play, reeled into consideration, neither in terms of postulating a hidden and yet to be a revealed dimension within the *Study*, nor in terms of a distinction to

Fernand Léger, *La Joconde aux Clés*, 1930, oil on canvas

be articulated in terms of representation and presentation, but as the crypt; the included enclosure. The *Studies*, the *mise en abyme*, is not silent. It is and is not what it cannot be. The *gl* that 'remarks what is shown as what is said,' does not reduce the remark to a surface. The *gl* is not a surface event. It cannot be enclosed by totalisation. Its totality refuses totality. It is at one and the same time a mark within the *Study* as well as the mark marking out in advance its resistance to absorption by either the phonic or the discursive. The 'remarque' and the 'retrait' are far from finished.

At one moment in this writing 'about' Derrida begins a paragraph with the following sentence;

The event is unnarratable [inénarrable] but the narrative [récit] moves on [s'enchaîne].

Whether this line is dragged from its context or relegated to its place in the chain of sentences comprising the text *+R (Into the Bargain)*, it can be seen as narrating the predicament of the encounter – within the ambit of heterogeneity – between philosophy and painting. In addition it recounts the situation of Derrida's writing about Adami. Here the 'about' can unfold *ad infinitum*. Derrida selected the threads he wished to pull. Equally I have followed some but not all of the threads, and that despite their pull. In

conclusion it must be added that there is no natural point at which to finish these deliberations. The preceeding is simply a presentation of aspects of Derrida's writing 'about' Adami. The *Study* is affirmed in its affirmation.

Interpreting / Painting and the Art of Deconstruction [41]

The challenge that shapes the need, if not the desire to interpret, when it is enacted within the frame of dominance, is inevitably marked by a form of perversity; as much cruel as pointless. The object thus interpreted is brought to order by order. The object is opened by an interpretive key. The truth of all interpretive objects is thought to be locked away and hidden from sight. The hidden truth – the *veritas abscondita* – positions the representation as itself the representation of a truth waiting to be discovered. Access to what waits is provided by a key. It will unlock the enigma. With its truth no longer hidden the enigma has been overcome. The object within interpretation is now the site of revelation, of unveiling. The key turning in the lock breaks the code's secret. The enigma decoded becomes a variety of truth rather than a variation from it.

Fernand Léger was fascinated by keys. Perhaps the fascination even spread to what they held. It is in one particular painting that the key comes face to face, not with an enigma but with a symbol. It is however not an enigmatic symbol but the symbol of enigma; *La Joconde*. The encounter takes place both within the frame as well as in its title; *La Joconde aux Clés*. A confrontation that circumscribes the interpretive situation. It is however a circumscription that has been inscribed within the frame.

Within what Derrida has identified as the logocentric tradition in philosophy the desire for mastery and domination cannot allow for a simple confrontation between key and enigma. There must be a resolution. In Adami's drawing, the fish on the hook is between life and death and yet it must either live or die. This uncertainty is unsupportable. And yet of course it is precisely this insupportable uncertainty that is supported by the line pulling the fish almost out of the almost-writing of what is taken to be *Glas*.

Léger's painting seems to proffer what, if the logic of interpretation is followed strictly, it cannot sustain. It presents the confrontation that is prior to interpretation. It has inscribed within the frame that practice of interpretation that is supposed to be 'of' the frame. The shift in prepositions is significant. It is as a consequence tempting to view the keys and *La Joconde* as constructing a *mise en abyme*. It is possible to go further and argue that they mark what here could be called the interpretive re-mark. This possibility opens a path that could be followed. Further arguments would need to be deployed in order to show how the *mise en abyme* was constructed and how the logic of the re-mark unfolded.

However, there remains the question of interpretation. Were the path to be followed along the lines suggested the question would in this instance take two forms. The first asks very simply, is not this attempt to show the impossibility of interpretation already an interpretation? In other words what has been offered thus far – the interpretation that calls interpretation into doubt – is this not a type of interpretation? The second asks with equal force, is this an interpretation? Here the question is more demanding since it is asking is what has been presented thus far an instance – albeit a schematic and introductory instance – of what in general is known as interpretation? The second question doubts. It is only by dwelling on these questions that it will then be possible to take up the challenge posed by the possibility of there being an art of deconstruction. It will be seen however that this possibility is enacted and undone by time.

At play in both these questions is a form of expectation. The expectation here is that the relationship between interpretation and object of interpretation involve compatibility. The language of the former will be compatible with the logic of the latter. Interpretive accord or homology will be therefore privileged over disaccord. It is exactly at this point that the difficulty emerges. Three specific though related points are raised by these questions.

The first point that must be noted is one that follows from Derrida's own argument concerning what has been called the architecture of affirmation. In sum it is that the traditional categories within philosophy and aesthetics are not able to express what is taking place within such an architecture. There is an inevitable disaccord. The strategy adopted by Derrida, Eisenman, Tschumi, etc., is to recognise this incompatibility and in so doing adopt different styles of writing and presentation (aphorisms, commentary, 'misreading', etc.) ones which while not aiming to express the architectural affirmation are nonetheless compatible with it. Here the possibility of compatibility involves an interplay or belonging together of the different rather than the banality of similitude taking place under the reign of the Same. The desire of logocentrism to offer

Gérard Titus-Carmel, *Suite Chancay, Varia no. 8*, 1985, ink on cloth

complete and all-encompassing explanations is rendered inoperable and inappropriate by what it seeks to describe. The object has a future that resists the finality of its incorporation into the act of interpretation. The holding apart as the holding together when taken as an approach to the affirmative provides the way for the development of an aesthetics opened up by deconstruction.

The next point involves the distinction – which may in fact be arbitrary – between the affirmative and the non-affirmative. This distinction can be deconstructed by the very fact that deconstruction is always already taking place. Even though that is the case there is nonetheless a difference between works which aspire to the totality and unity outlined, if not decreed, in advance by logocentrism, and which therefore desire to be compatible with its interpretive apparatus, and those which in their very articulation of their work recognise and affirm the impossibility of the metaphysics of presence and totality. Affirmation however is not the result of following a programme. Affirmation involves the maintenance, but displacement, of teleology.

The final point returns to the questions posed above. There is no sense in which it is being argued that Léger is a deconstructive artist; or indeed that *La Joconde aux Clés* is a deconstructive painting. (Nor for that matter is an argument being advanced for the opposite position). The reason why this has to be the case is presented by Geoff Bennington within a more general claim about Derrida's philosophical project:

> Deconstruction is not a theory or a project. It does not prescribe a practice more or less faithful to it, nor project an image of a desirable state to be brought about.[42]

What took place in the preceeding discussion of *La Joconde aux Clés* was an attempt to trace within its frame the impossibility of fulfilling what is demanded by interpretation as totality. The key and the enigma are held together but the enigma remains and the key has not opened the object of interpretation, which is after all the painting *La Joconde aux Clés*. The painting as object of interpretation contains the possibility of interpretation and the impossibility of interpretation. It must rid itself of what it has if the logocentric aspiration for totality is to endure and yet it is exactly this element that sanctions interpretation. Interpretation is checked, stopped by that which made it possible.

Interpretation therefore divides between totality and the recognition of its impossibility. However this does not mean that the language and categories of conventional aesthetic theory or interpretation are cast aside. It has already been argued in relation to Descartes and Eisenman that this is an impossible state of affairs. That which dominated is housed within what emerges as the consequences of its no longer being able to dominate. The rewriting of interpretation in terms of domination and affirmation brings to the fore a further divide.

The desire for domination resulted in an incompatability between concepts and painting. The frame as the site of heterogeneity was not compatible with concepts and theories inscribed within and thus demanding the Same. The irony is that the recognition of the essential incompatibility of painting and writing about painting allows for a different type of compatibility. It becomes rewritten in terms of the belonging together of the different. Expressed in this way it recalls the point noted earlier by David Carrol. He argued that Derrida 'mobilises' art and theory in such a way as to allow for them to be rethought in terms of the 'frames that both separate them and link them together.' While Carrol is absolutely right in his description, what is lacking is the attempt to distinguish between the affirmative and the non-affirmative. While it is true, as

a number of commentators have argued and indeed as has been argued above, that the frame, like the text, contains heterogeneity, there is still a distinction between the affirmative and those works engaging and thereby rehearsing 'nihilistic repetition' (while there can be no deconstructive programme in art). This is true only in the sense that deconstruction cannot identify in advance – and hence programme – art itself. However this does not mean that there are not painters, as there are writers and philosophers, whose work takes place within what can be called the deconstruction of metaphysics. If fundamental to that particular philosophical enterprise is the timely attempt to rethink history such that it is no longer seen as an external touchstone grounding interpretation, then it becomes possible to situate the paintings of Anselm Kiefer within such an enterprise. Furthermore if the deconstruction of teleology means that paintings may inscribe within their presentation an affirmative break between painting and vision (to shorten the argument to come it will be assumed that vision provides the dominant telos of painting), then it is possible to situate the paintings of Cy Twombly within such an undertaking. It will be in terms of Kiefer and Twombly that it will be possible to link deconstruction and an art of affirmation; the link both joins and overlaps.

There is an obvious preliminary problem concerning the attribution of affirmation; in sum it involves how to understand the refusal of repetition. The specificity of that refusal will always be paramount. However the painting will not portray that refusal. It is rather that the painting will demand an explanation/interpretation/reading (it is almost possible to allow these terms to proliferate *ad infinitum*) for which the categories are not at hand. Here it is possible to speak of the avant-guard. (In addition, and in a different mode, here is the point of connection between deconstruction and the work of Jean-François Lyotard in regard to the field of painting). If then the painting is not an exemplification of refusal how is affirmation to be understood? The general answer to this question has already been given. Affirmation means the refusal of repetition and thus with the subsequent rethinking to which that refusal gives space. It is the generality of such a response that limits its force. Situating the general will take place via a brief consideration of Twombly and Kiefer.

If understanding what is intended by affirmation can be taken a step further by looking at Cy Twombly it is because of what is at play in 'looking'. Roland Barthes in *Cy*

Above: Cy Twombly, *Mars and the Artist*, 1975, oil, chalk, charcoal and pencil on paper
Below: Cy Twombly, *Virgil*, 1973, oil and chalk on paper

Above: Anselm Kiefer, *Painting = Burning*, 1974, oil on burlap
Below: Anselm Kiefer, *Icarus – March Sand*, 1981, oil, emulsion, shellac, and sand on photograph, on canvas

Twombly ou Non multa sed multum[43] draws attention to the role of the eye both within painting and the history of thought. It is not just that the eye sees, it is also that sight forms a significant part of the history of philosophy. It plays a fundamental role in rationalism (Cartesian clear and distinct perception), empiricism (Berkeley's *esse est percipi*), resemblance (Hume and the relationship between ideas and impressions). Derrida has taken great care in connecting logocentrism within the privileging of the eye and sight. (The ocularcentric). The interrelationship between the eye, sight, vision and logocentrism has been emphasised by both Barthes and Derrida.

There is an additional element here, namely that this interrelationship plays a pivotal role in establishing the telos of painting. Painting is to be seen. Its own clarity – even the clarity of its obscurity – works to intertwine painting and vision; vision becoming the end of painting. For Barthes all of these elements are combines in what he calls 'a repressive rationality'. It is in connection to this repression that Twombly's work appears disruptive. Barthes interprets it as breaking the interrelationship between, the eye, vision, sight and painting, and in so doing it liberates 'painting from vision', and, it can be added, from vision as the telos of painting. Barthes' text on Twombly can be read as an interpretation of the affirmative.

The parameters of Barthes' interpretation – some cursory elements which have been sketched here – indicate the specificity of affirmation. The writing within Twombly's work, the fact that it deploys what Barthes describes as 'les scrawls des enfants', its 'blindness', its resistance to what painting would seem to demand (both of itself and interpretation), serve to indicate how, what Barthes describes as a liberation demands an interpretive strategy and terminology that is appropriate to the object itself. Indeed it must be an interpretation that sustains a terminology that can express the 'liberation' without reducing it to a simple act of deviance or defiance. Indeed this is the strength and the importance of Barthes' and Derrida's terminological innovations. They are innovations demanded by the work, and in Barthes' case often specific to it. The development of a terminology enacts, on the one hand, the maintenance of heterogeneity, while on the other it announces the refusal of repetition. While deconstruction is always already taking place within the work of art, the heterogeneity of Twombly is not masked by the pretence of presenting the culmination of painting's telos. Their 'scrawl' is more demanding.

Anselm Kiefer's paintings present a more difficult problem. They bring with them the burden of history as well as the possibility of memory. Memory and history raise the question of time. Time is already in play. The use of the expression 'always already' works to undermine the possibility of the programme, because it defines the heterogeneous as original: hence no deconstructive art but hence the art of deconstruction. Here time plays a different role.

In discussing the roles of time and space within Kiefer's work, Irit Rogoff brings up the relationship between history and time in her analysis of *Iconoclastic Controversy*:

> Politics here are the agent of the symbolic occupation which both nature and culture have been forced to undergo. Within this occupation that ancient past, the recent past and the efforts at deliverance made by the artist/palette are all synthesised within a non-historical time.[44]

On one level a great deal of Kiefer's work concerns an attempt to dwell on the past; a specific past; Germany's past. However what does it mean to dwell on the past? What is the time of this dwelling?

Painting = Burning, 1974, checks both in its title and within its frame any automatic attempt to construe the work of art as revelation. All that is revealed is that which refuses representation; the Holocaust, nuclear annihilation, the remains of the after war. They are not events in history for they have called into question the very process that is the making of history. The means of representation – the palette – becomes a mere outline announcing the impossibility of placing on the canvas that which the burning removed. It is the emptiness of the palette that announces in advance the vacuity of history.

It is empty precisely because the annihilation while inscribed within and made possible by the history of domination cannot be represented by that history. In other words the events of annihilation explicable in terms of cultures, bodies of thought, artistic practices, that have privileged representation as presence (presence as representation), cannot be represented within that of which they form an integral part. The breakdown of representation coupled to the impossibility of pure presence means that the trace which while working to produce presence does at the same time engender conception of, for example, symbol/icon/emblem/representation that no longer locates and restricts meaning to the relationship between symbols and symbolised, representation and reality etc.[45]

The empty palette – the palette as outline, as trace – also figures within more recent paintings, where it is joined to wings. In *Palette with Wings*, 1981, the winged palette is painted over a photograph of a deserted and perhaps ruined place. In *Icarus – March Sand*, 1981, the palette seems to fly across a field. These palettes are deployed in other paintings, ones whose titles directly refer to German mythology or history. The question in each instance, though specifically in relation to these two paintings, is what type of distance or gap is established by the palette's flight? There are many different and incompatible answers to this question. It may be, for example, that flight could be explained in terms of transcendence. Flight may signal the purported supremacy of art. Furthermore art could have become a shelter. It would seem however that each of the possibilities is undermined by the title *Icarus – March Sand*. If art were simply transcendent then it would become untenable. It could not be both transcendent and collapse. Rather than try and understand the gap established by flight as making a claim about art that isolates the palette, could it not be that this distance – this separation – is precisely a gap, a separation, a distance? The holding apart is what is essential. It is not the sign of loss but of the impossibility of recovery. This impossibility of figures within the possibility of art. It is thus that his paintings are neither historical (in the conventional sense) nor nostalgic.

In a recent discussion of his work Maureen Sherlock has tried to link him to Heidegger:

> Like Heidegger, Kiefer's reappraisal of history is offered as an overcoming of the forgetfulness of the present and the restoration of a more remote and authentic past.[46]

Independently of whether or not this is an accurate interpretation of Heidegger, what is nonetheless enacted by the analogy is an interpretation of Kiefer's work within the very temporality that it seeks to deny. The 'overcoming of forgetfulness' would reconnect the present with the past. The place within which this happened would be the work of art. The artist's task would therefore be delimited by, and therefore restricted to, the enactment of this overcoming. It is not just that this possibility is only possible within an historical conception of time – time as chronological – it would also demand a full palette. Finally any attempt to recover the past, especially a past that is more 'authentic' is contingent upon a certain conception of the symbol. It must restore by its capacity to refer. The painting therefore would have been enacted within representation. However it has already been suggested that it is Kiefer's sensitivity to history that renders such a procedure impossible. Within his work symbols both refer and do not refer. The meaning of the symbol is not restricted to that semantic place defined by the relation between symbol and symbolised; other meanings are possible.

Kiefer is concerned with the history of this possibility. It is displayed in *Painting = Burning*. Here, it can be argued, is an attempt to think historically while recognising firstly the impossibility of symbols to function within the restricted semantic and interpretive realm they demand, and secondly the impossibility of there being a narrative of complete inclusion, since the desire for totality not only excludes annihilation, annihilation cannot be represented within it. The narrative of history as inclusion not only has its own architectonic but involves a temporality of finitude. Kiefer's dwelling on history sustains an open response. This sustained opening allows for what cannot be predicted. The temporality at play here echoes that of the 'always already'. In the same way as it refused a beginning, an *arché*, the sustained opening refuses finitude. A different conception of temporality is necessary. It is not just that historical time – the temporality of the narrative of inclusion – is no longer deployed. It is rather that the time of the history of metaphysics, representation and domination, has becomes displaced. Such a time is inappropriate. *Painting = Burning* cannot be articulated within it. As a work of art it demands rethinking. It can only ever be transgressed by the attempt to include it within the dominion of the Same. These comments have concerned only one of Kiefer's works. They could perhaps provide an approach to *March Heath*, 1974, then to *Father, Son, Holy Ghost*, 1973.

Twombly and Kiefer despite their differences, though perhaps because of them, can be understood as affirmative. The works alluded to above can be seen as resisting and refusing 'nihilistic repetition'. Two related possibilities emerge here, one is a politics of deconstruction and the other is the art of deconstruction. They are of course both always already the other.

NOTES

Deconstruction, Post-Modernism and the Visual Arts by Christopher Norris

1 See especially Jacques Derrida, *Of Grammatology*, trans. Gayatri C. Spivak, Johns Hopkins University Press, Baltimore, 1976.
2 Derrida, 'Plato's Pharmacy', in *Dissemination*, trans. Barbara Johnson, Athlone Press, London, 1981, pp. 61-171.
3 Derrida, 'Nature, Culture, Writing', in *Of Grammatology* (op. cit.), pp. 95-316.
4 See Claude Lévi-Strauss, *Tristes Tropiques*, trans. John and Doreen Weightman, Cape, London, 1973.
5 Ferdinand de Saussure, *Course in General Linguistics*, trans. Wade Baskin, Cape, London, 1974.
6 See Derrida, 'Differance', in *'Speech And Phenomena' and Other Essays on Husserl's Theory of Signs*, trans. David B. Allison, Northwestern University Press, Evanston, 1973, pp. 129-60.
7 Derrida, *Edmund Husserl's 'Origin of Geometry': an introduction*, trans. John P. Leavey, Duquesne University Press, Pittsburgh, 1978.
8 On this topic see especially Gilles Deleuze, *Kant's Critical Philosophy: the doctrine of the faculties*, trans. Hugh Tomlinson and Barbara Habberjam, Athlone Press, London, 1984.
9 See also Kant's notoriously elusive passage on the 'productive imagination' in *Critique of Pure Reason*, trans. F. Max Müller, Macmillan, New York, 1922, p. 116.
10 On this topic see Paul Crowther, 'Beyond Art and Philosophy: deconstruction and the postmodern sublime', in 'The New Modernism', *Art and Design*, Academy Editions, London, Vol 4, No 3/4, 1988, pp. 47-52.
11 The best account of these Kantian elements in Derrida's thought may be found in Rodolphe Gasché, *The Tain of the Mirror: Derrida and the philosophy of reflection*, Harvard University Press, Cambridge, Mass, 1986.
12 See the numerous examples of this prejudice cited in Derrida, *Of Grammatology* (op. cit.), pp. 6-93.
13 See Derrida, 'The Pit and the Pyramid: introduction to Hegel's semiology', in *Margins of Philosophy*, trans. Alan Bass, University of Chicago Press, Chicago, 1982, pp. 69-108.
14 Derrida, *Glas*, trans. John P. Leavey and Richard Rand, University of Nebraska Press, Lincoln and London, 1986.
15 On this topic see also Derrida, *Signéponge*, trans. Richard Rand, Columbia University Press, New York, 1984.
16 Hegel, *Phenomenology of Spirit*, trans. A.V. Miller, Oxford University Press, Oxford, 1977.
17 Derrida, *Glas* (op. cit.), p. 50.
18 Derrida, *The Truth in Painting*, trans. Geoff Bennington and Ian McLeod, University of Chicago Press, Chicago, 1987. All further references given by *TP* and page number in the text.
19 See Martin Heidegger, 'The Origin of the Work of Art', in *Poetry, Language, Thought*, trans. Albert Hofstadter, Harper & Row, New York, 1971, pp. 17-87. His discussion of the Van Gogh painting may be found at pp. 32-7.
20 Derrida, *De l'esprit: Heidegger et la question*, Galilée, Paris, 1987.
21 See Derrida, *Of Grammatology* (op. cit.), p. 99.
22 Plato, *The Republic*, trans. H.D.P. Lee, Penguin, Harmondsworth, 1955, pp. 278-86.
23 Derrida, 'The Double Session', in *Dissemination* (op. cit.), pp. 173-286.
24 ibid., p. 199.
25 ibid., pp. 206-7.
26 See the essays collected in Walter Benjamin, *Illuminations*, ed. Hannah Arendt, Fontana, London, 1973.
27 Derrida, *Dissemination* (op. cit.), p. 193.
28 Walter Benjamin, 'The Work of Art in the Age of Mechanical Reproduction', in *Illuminations* (op. cit.), pp. 219-53.
29 See for instance Derrida, 'The Principle of Reason: the university in the eyes of its pupils', in *Diacritics*, Vol. XIX, 1983, pp. 3-20.
30 See Kant, *The Conflict of the Faculties*, trans. & ed. Mary Gregor, Abaris Books, New York, 1979.
31 Derrida, 'The Principle of Reason' (op. cit.), p. 13.
32 Derrida, 'Fifty-Two Aphorisms for a Foreword', trans. Andrew Benjamin, Tate Gallery/Academy Forum, London, 1988. Two-page document published as symposium material: all further references here given in the text.
33 See Derrida, 'The Principle of Reason' (op. cit.).
34 Derrida, 'Force and Signification', in *Writing and Difference*, trans. Alan Bass, Routledge & Kegan Paul, London, 1978, pp. 1-30.
35 ibid., p. 26.
36 For an informative (if barbed) exchange on these topics, see Eisenman's interview with Charles Jencks in 'Deconstruction in Architecture', *Architectural Design*, Vol 58, No 3/4, Academy Editions, London, 1988, pp. 49-61. See also Derrida, 'Point de folie – maintenant l'architecture' and 'Pourquoi Peter Eisenman écrit de si bons livres', in *Psyché: inventions de l'autre*, Galilée, Paris, 1987, pp. 477-93; 495-508.
37 Peter Eisenman, 'The Blue Line Text' (typescript copy).
38 Derrida, 'White Mythology: metaphor in the text of philosophy', in *Margins of Philosophy* (op. cit.), pp. 207-71.
39 ibid., p. 228.
40 ibid., p. 229.
41 See for instance Jean-François Lyotard, *The Postmodern Condition: a report on knowledge*, trans. Geoff Bennington and Brian Massumi, University of Minnesota Press, Minneapolis, 1983.
42 For a useful discussion and extended bibliography see Linda Hutcheon, 'Beginning to Theorise Postmodernism', in *Textual Practice*, Vol. I, No. 1, 1987, pp. 10-31.
43 As indeed they are for an avowedly 'postmodern' philosopher like Richard Rorty. See his essay 'Philosophy as a Kind of Writing', in *Consequences Of Pragmatism*, University of Minnesota Press, Minneapolis, 1981, pp. 90-109.
44 Fredric Jameson, 'Postmodernism, or the Cultural Logic of Late Capitalism', in *New Left Review*, No. 146, 1984, pp. 53-92.
45 See for instance Terry Eagleton's response to Jameson, ' Capitalism, Modernism and Postmodernism', in *New Left Review*, No. 152, 1985, pp. 60-73.
46 Charles Jencks, 'Deconstruction: the pleasures of absence', in *Architectural Design*, (op. cit.), pp. 17-31.
47 See Charles Jencks, *Post-Modernism: the new classicism in art and architecture*, Academy Editions, London, 1987.
48 Bernard Tschumi, 'Parc de la Villette, Paris', in *Architectural Design* (op. cit.), pp. 33-39.
49 Derrida, *Dissemination* (op. cit.), p. 207.

Deconstruction and Art / The Art of Deconstruction by Andrew Benjamin

1 Derrida refers to the 'itself' of deconstruction in *Memoires for Paul de Man*, trans. by C. Lindsay, J. Culler and E. Cadava, Columbia University Press, New York, 1986.
2 In *Derrida and Différance*, edited by D. Wood and R. Bernasconi, trans. by D. Wood, A. Benjamin, Northwestern University Press, Evanston, 1988.
3 Dodds draws this distinction in his edition of the *Georgias*, Oxford University Press, 1979, p. 193.
4 The relationship between Being and Becoming is one of the most important philosophical questions. While it should not be expressed in terms of

an either/or, the question seems to resolve itself either in Heidegger's direction where becoming is viewed as an expression of Being, or in Nietzsche where the relationship between them marks a fundamental antagonism. There is more at stake here than can be provided in a simple summation.

5 R. Gasché, *The Tain of the Mirror*, Harvard University Press, Cambridge, 1986, pp. 177-255. My treatment of deconstruction has been significantly influenced by Gasché's interpretation. I find it the most sophisticated philosophical treatment of deconstruction thus far.

6 D. Carroll, *Paraesthetics*, Methuen, New York, 1987, p. 144.

7 In *Margins of Philosophy*, trans. by Paul Bass, Routledge and Kegan Paul, London, 1985.

8 I. Harvey, *Derrida and the Economy of Différance*, Indiana University Press, Bloomington, 1986, p. 112.

9 J. Llewelyn, *Derrida and the Threshold of Sense*, Macmillan, London, 1986, p. 83.

10 *Ulysse gramaphone*, Galilée, Paris, 1987, p. 40.

11 J. Derrida, *Signéponge*, Editions de Seuil, Paris, 1988.

12 The affirmative refers to what he called a Nietzschean element within deconstruction. It will be discussed in greater detail in parts III and IV.

13 Derrida, *Memoires for Paul de Man* (op. cit.), p. 73. C. Norris has written an important overview of Derrida's work on de Man, 'The Rhetoric of Remembrance; Derrida on de Man', in *Textual Practice*, Vol 1, No 2, 1987.

14 J. Derrida, 'Cinquant-deux aphorisms pour un avant-propos', in *Psyché*, Galilée, Paris, 1988, p. 513.

15 Derrida makes precisely this point in the following terms:

De-construction analyses and compares conceptual pairs, which are currently accepted as self-evident and natural as if they had not been institutionalised at some precise moment, as if they had no history. Because of being taken for granted they restrict thinking.

J. Derrida, 'Architetture ove il desidrio può abitare', *Domus*, No 671, April 1986. Furthermore Eisenman's critique of modernism involves a similar type of argument:

Modernism in proclaiming function to be the essence of architecture, proposed to elevate the classical metaphysic of architecture to the status of natural law.

P. Eisenman, *The House of Cards*, Oxford University Press, New York, 1988, p. 189.

16 Bernard Tschumi, 'Parc de la Villette, Paris', in *Architectural Design*, Academy Editions, London, Vol 58, No 3/4, 1988, p. 38.

17 Derrida (op. cit.).

18 I have discussed Descartes' architectural 'metaphor' in greater detail in 'Derrida, Philosophy and Architecture', in *Architectural Design*, Vol 58, No 3/4, 1988.

19 M. Heidegger, *Basic Writings*, trans. by D. F. Krell, Routledge and Kegan Paul, London 1978, p. 323.

20 H. Fujii, Ushimade International Arts Festival, 1985, in *Architectural Design*, Vol 58, No 5/6, 1988, p. 48.

21 B. Tschumi (op. cit.).

22 P. Eisenman, *The House of Cards*, Oxford University Press, New York, 1988.

23 ibid., p. 185.

24 The importance of repetition (and with it tradition) cannot be overemphasised. It is in terms of repetiton that the distinction between Eisenman and Descartes can be understood. Repetition provides a key for understanding the ineliminable trait. In addition Derrida makes use of repetition in order to indicate the disruptive force of Tschumi's *Folies*; for Derrida they are not entrapped by 'the secretly nihilistic repetition of metaphysical architecture'. J. Derrida, 'Point de Folie', trans. by Kate Linker, in *AA Files*, No 12, 1986. For a recent attempt to rethink repetition from within a philosophical perspective influenced by Derrida see J. Caputo, *Radical Hermeneutics*, Indiana University Press, Bloomington, 1987. The major work in this area is still G. Deleuze, *Différence et Répétition*, P.U.F., France, 1969.

25 P. Eisenman (op. cit.) p. 169.

26 ibid., p. 169.

27 in *Digraphe*, No 11, 1977, see p. 103.

28 Derrida, 'Point de Folie' (op. cit.), p. 69.

29 For examples of some of this work see P. Johnson and M. Wigley, *Deconstructivist Architecture*, Museum of Modern Art, New York, 1988.

30 J. Derrida, *The Truth in Painting*, (hereafter TP) trans. by G. Bennington and I. McLeod, University of Chicago Press, Chicago, 1987, p. 10. Reference will at times be made to the French text, *La Vérité en Peinture*, Flammarion, Paris, 1978.

31 Adami has attracted considerable philosophical and theoretical interest in France. See in particular H. Damisch, *Fenêtre jaune cadmium*, Editions de Seuil, Paris, 1984, pp. 240-73, and Jean-Francois Lyotard, 'Anamnesis of the Visible, Or: Candour', in *The Lyotard Reader*, ed. A. Benjamin, Blackwells, Oxford, (forthcoming 1989).

32 J. Derrida, 'Fors' which is the preface to N. Abraham and M. Torok, *Cryptonymie, Le Verbier de L'Homme aux Loups*, Aubier Flammarion, Paris, 1976. The problematic of the crypt is also discussed by Derrida in 'Scribble (writing-power)', *Yale French Studies*, 59, 1979.

33 Derrida seems to warn against a too hasty generalisation of the crypt. Its complexity precludes any easy summation. What is at stake here is a philosophical practice beyond the domination of either representation or mimesis; hence the crypt and hence the *mise en abyme*.

34 *TP*, p.155.

35 J. Derrida, *Signéponge/Signsponge*, trans. R. Rand, Columbia University Press, New York, 1984, p. 155.

36 J. Llewelyn, *Derrida on the Threshold of Sense*, p. 71. Llewelyn's book reproduces the χ on its front cover, a mark it would be worth pursuing.

37 G. Bennington, 'Deconstruction is Not What You Think', in *Art & Design*, Vol 4, No 3/4, 1988, p. 7.

38 The relationship between Derrida and Heidegger gives rise to problems which are at the same time partisan and important. Gasché has argued in a number of places for the incompatibility of their philosophical projects. Other philosophers, notably John Sallis, see a fundamental affinity between them. See J. Sallis, 'Heidegger/Derrida – presence', in *Delimitations*, Indiana University Press, Bloomington, 1986. The relationship and the problems it raises do not give rise to an easy resolution. It is not a simple matter of choice. In the long run, however, the possibility of a resolution will turn on how the philosophical task is both construed and enacted within their work.

39 *TP*, p. 159.

40 R. Gasché, *The Tain of the Mirror*, p. 212.

41 There would seem to be some need for a warning or a defensive gesture that would try to extricate deconstruction from – as well as to implicate it in – the proceeding (in addition to proceeding). Derrida has not addressed the topics dealt with in this section. Or at least not addressed them in a way that allows for 'his own' position to be summarised. Even this way of expressing the problem is marked by difficulties. I am making no claims about what Derrida would or would not sanction. I am merely deploying an understanding of deconstruction within the field of interpreting/painting.

42 G. Bennington, 'Deconstruction is Not What You Think' (op. cit.), p. 7.

43 in R. Barthes. *L'obvie et l'obtus*, Edition du Seuil, Paris 1982. For reasons of space I have not really done justice to the richness of Barthes' text. I would add however that Barthes' continual attempt to find a language in which to write about painting needs to be understood within the ambit of the deconstruction of metaphysics.

44 I. Rogoff, 'Representations of Politics; Critics, Pessimists, Radicals', in *German Art in the 20th Century*, ed. C. M. Joachimides, N. Rosenthal, W. Schmied, Royal Academy of Arts, London, 1985, p. 132.

45 It is in just these terms that it would be necessary to begin an interpretation of Julian Schnabel's painting *God*.

46 M. Sherlock, 'Romancing the Apocalypse', *New Art Examiner*, Vol. 15, No. 10, 1988, p. 27.